T0171323

Katie's Doodles

ADVANCED COLORING BOOK

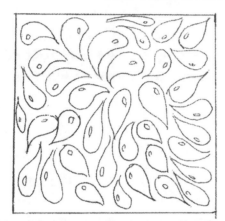
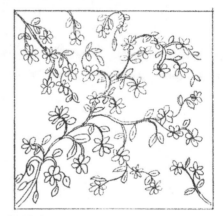

KATIE PIPRUDE

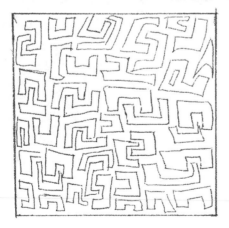
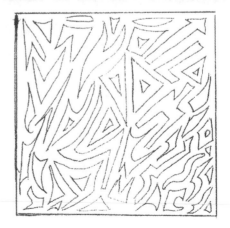

authorHOUSE®

AuthorHouse™
1663 Liberty Drive
Bloomington, IN 47403
www.authorhouse.com
Phone: 1-800-839-8640

First published by AuthorHouse 7/1/2009

ISBN: 978-1-4389-5806-4 (sc)

Printed in the United States of America
Bloomington, Indiana

This book is printed on acid-free paper.

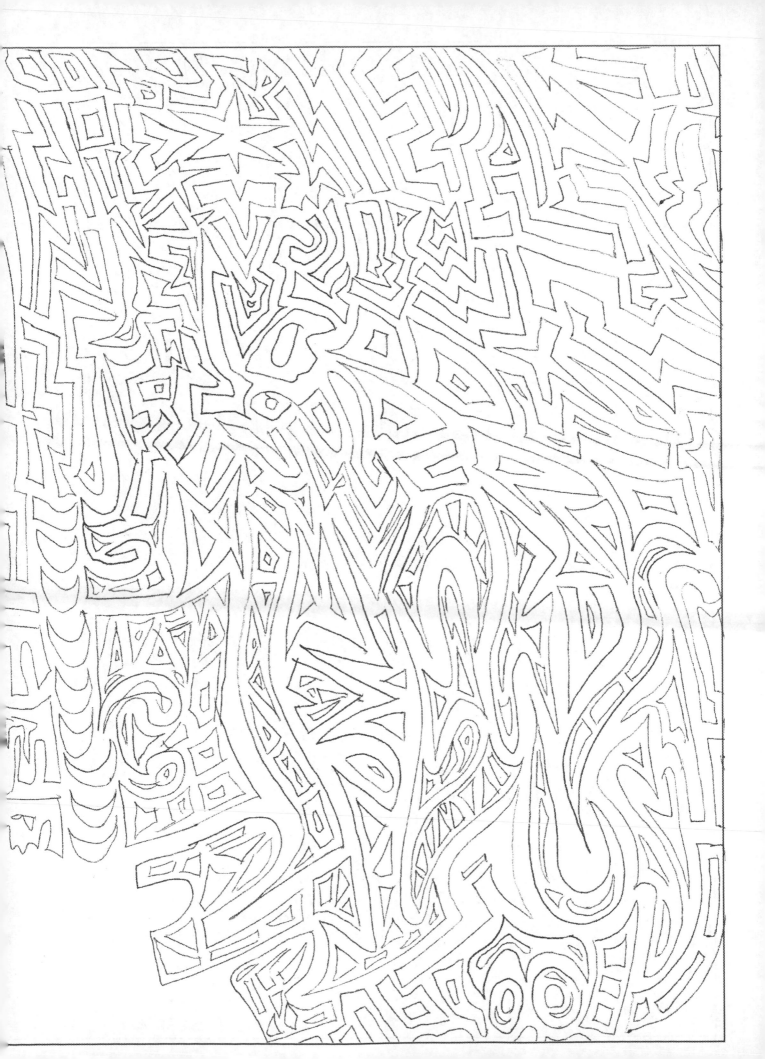

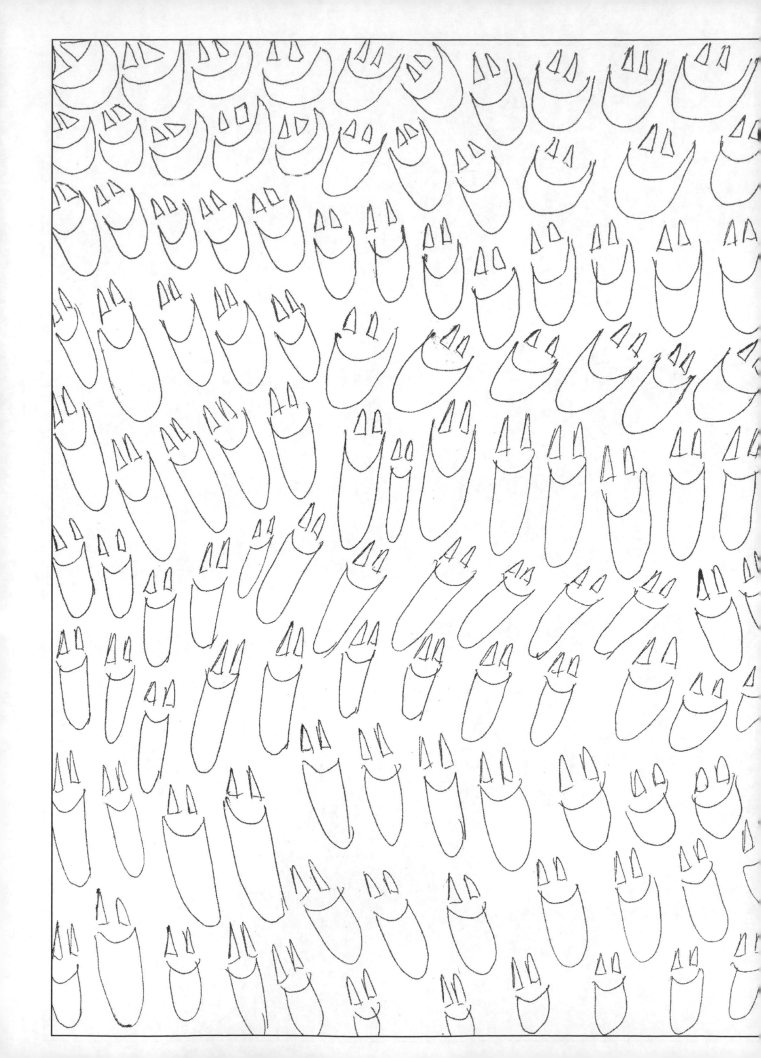

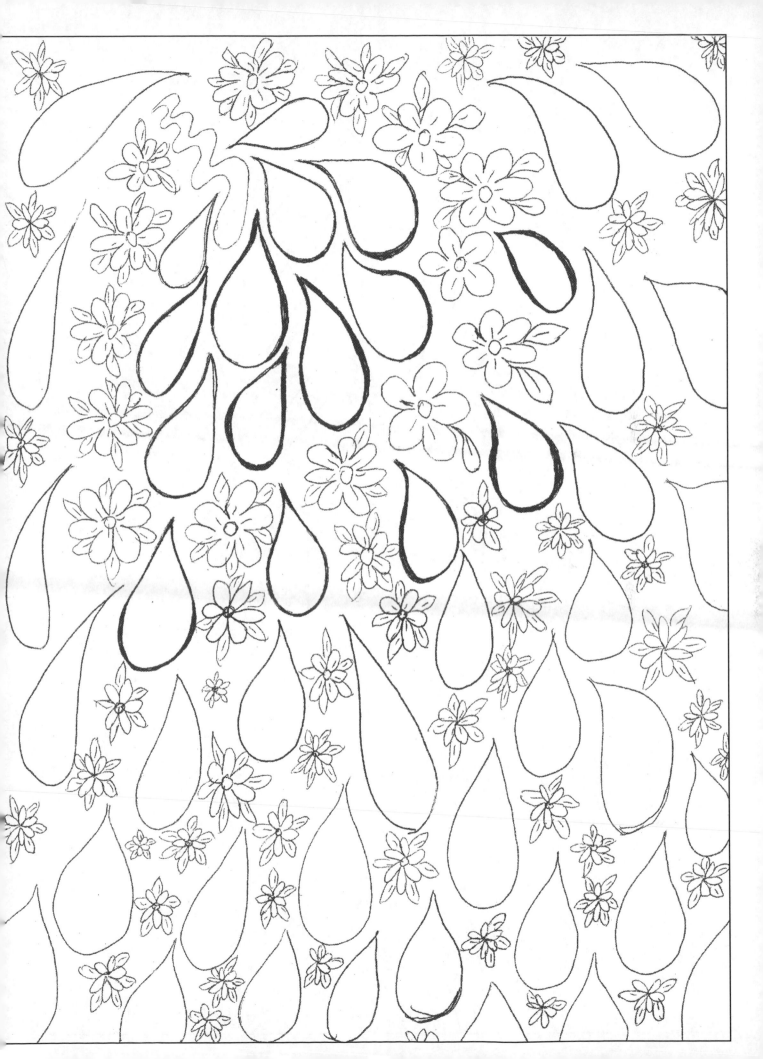

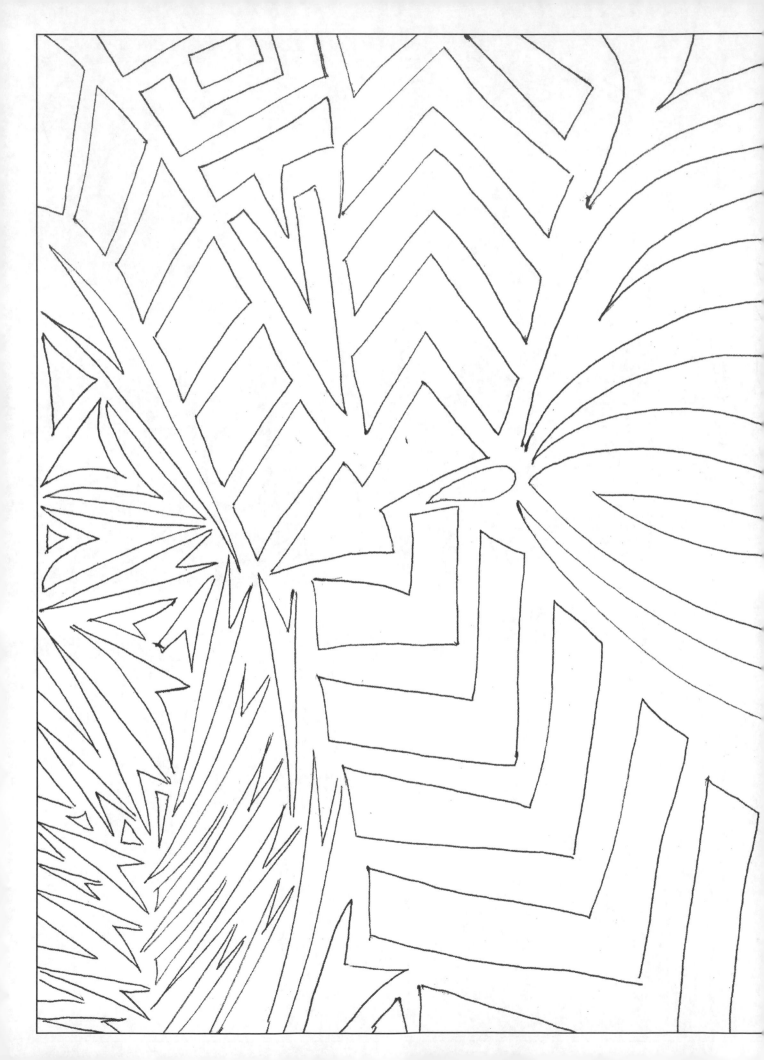

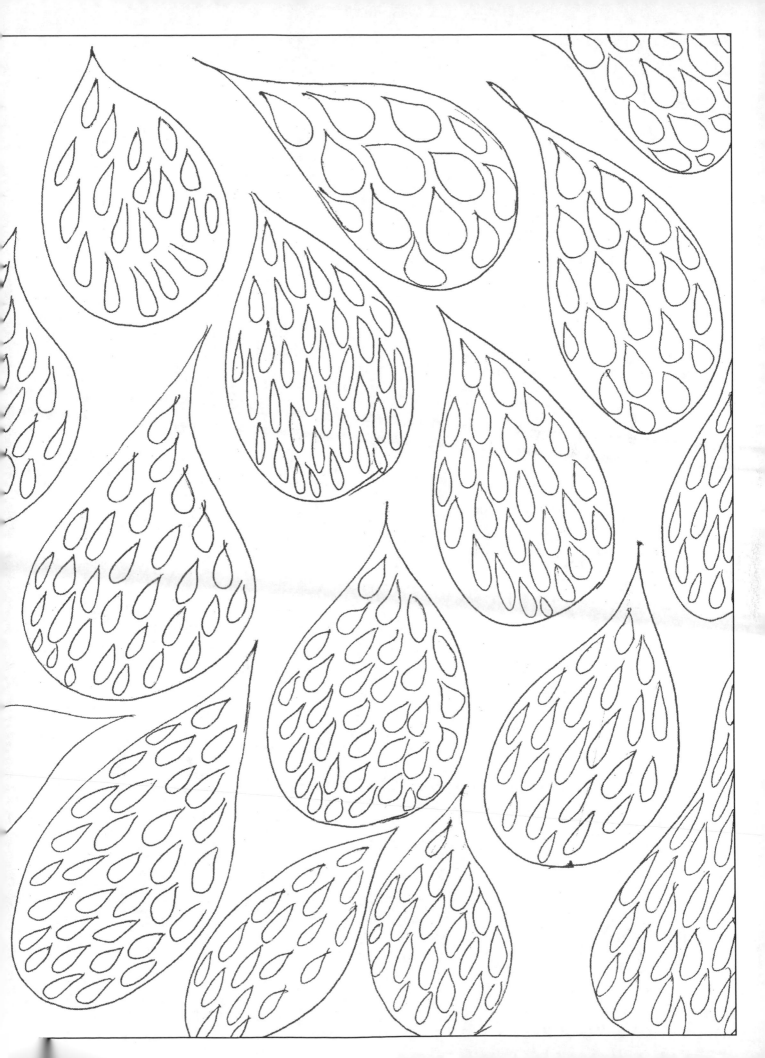

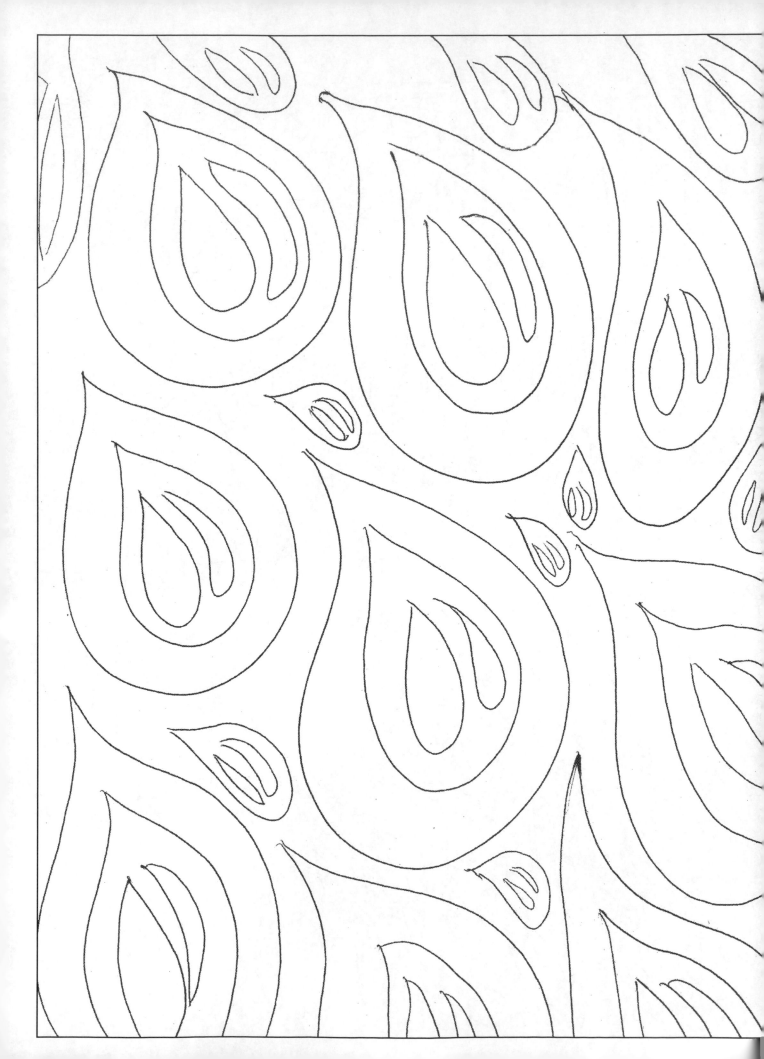

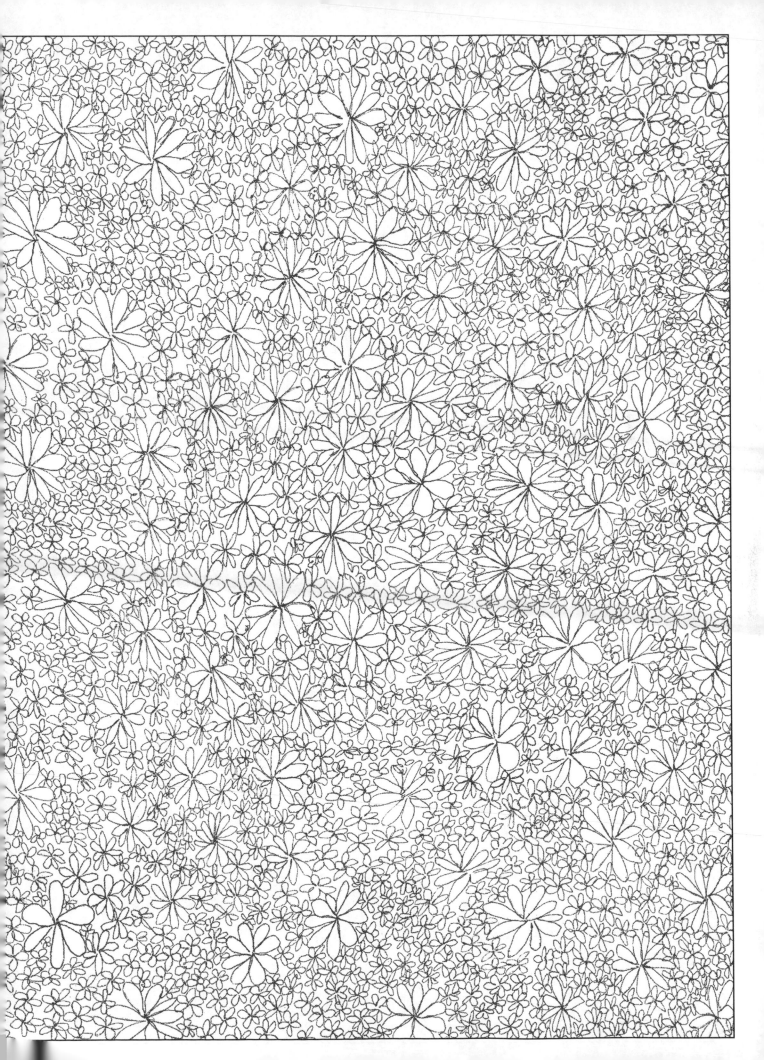

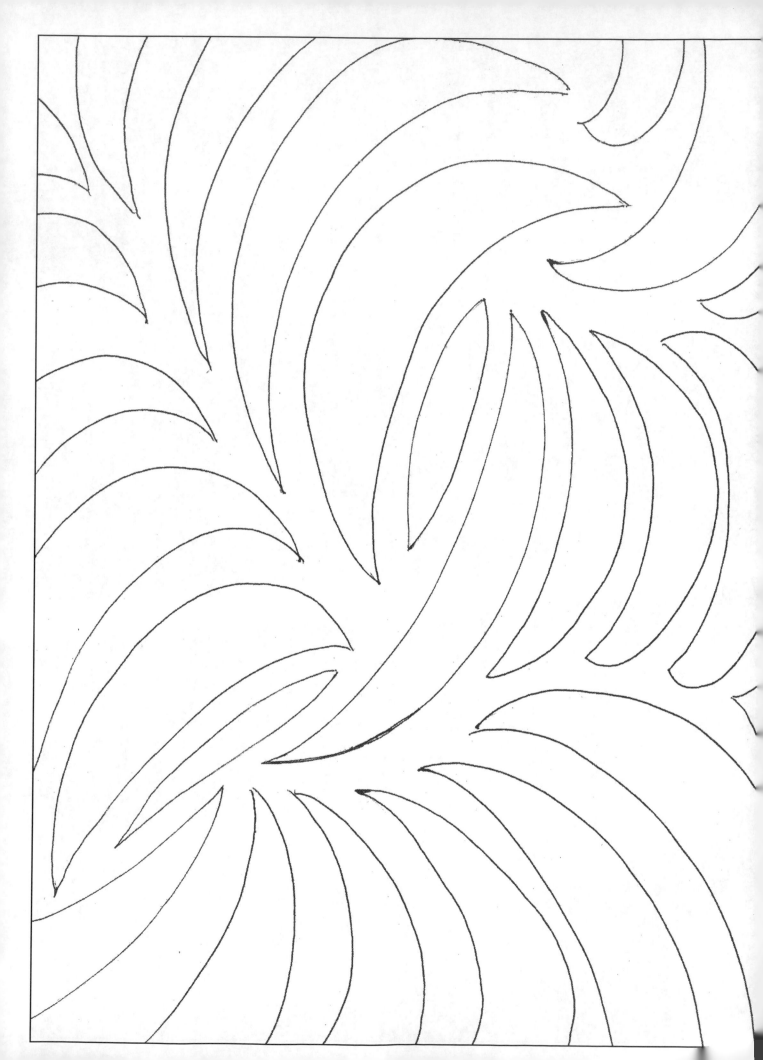

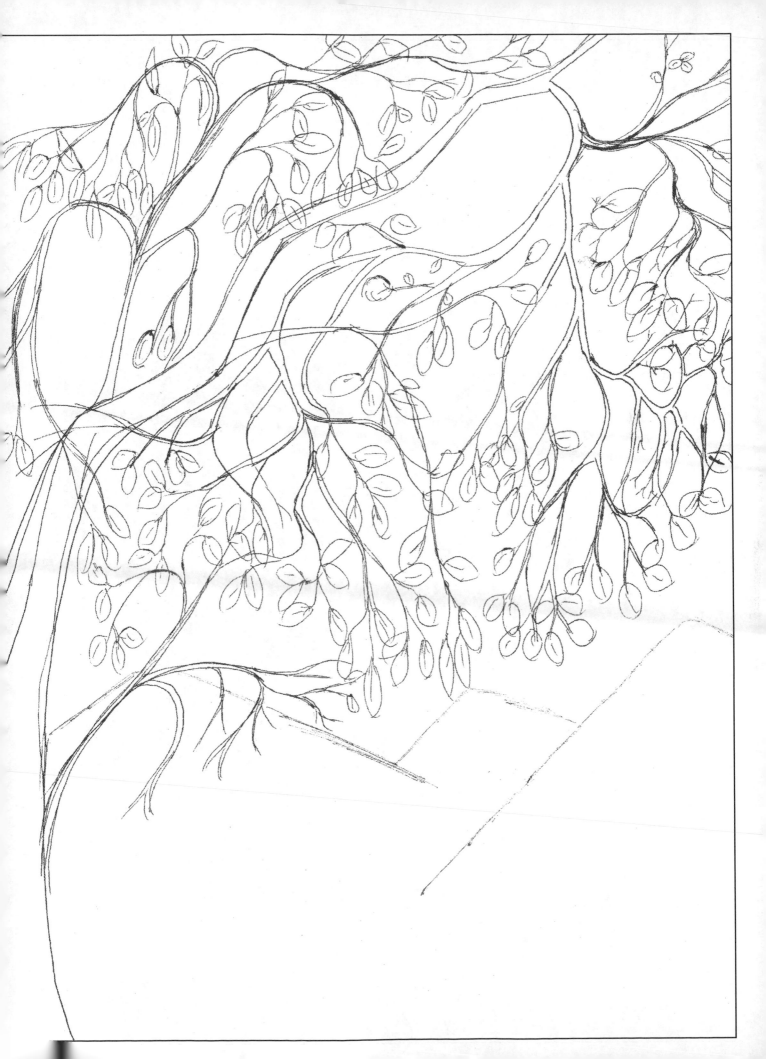

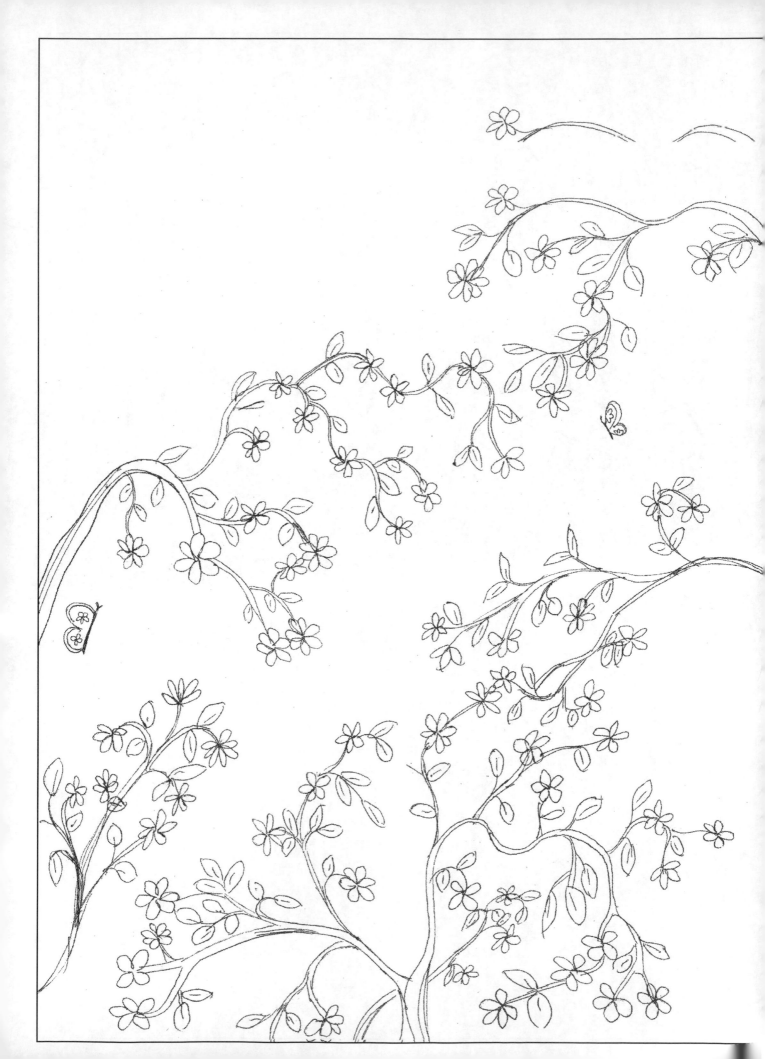

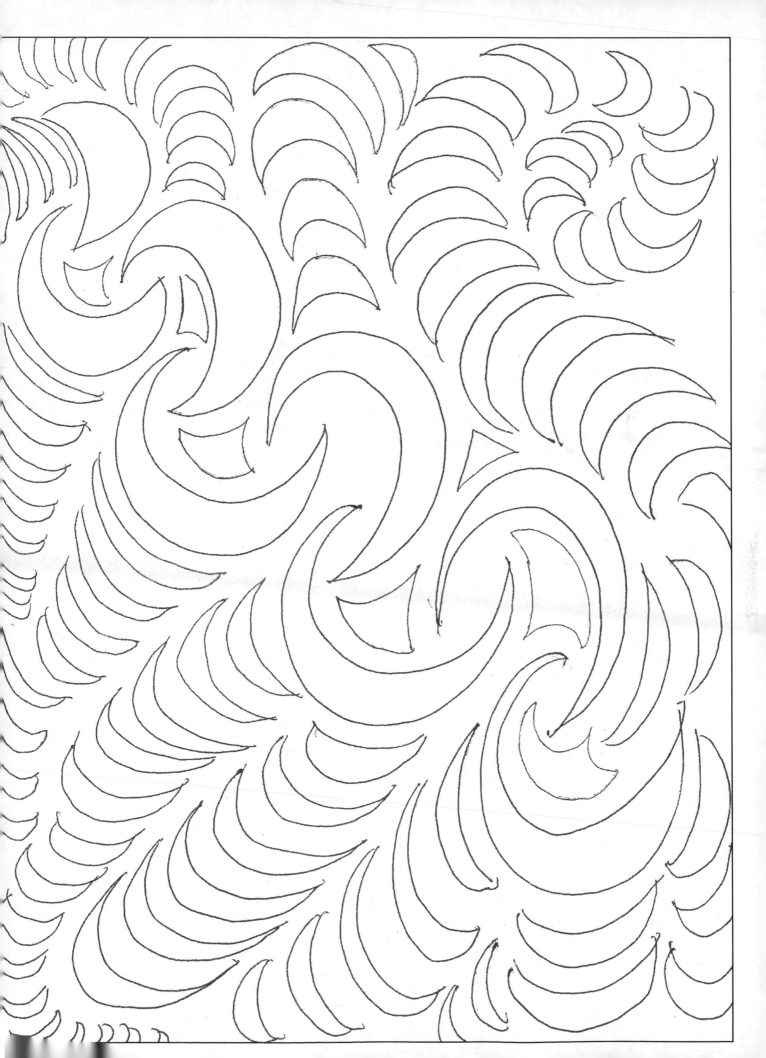

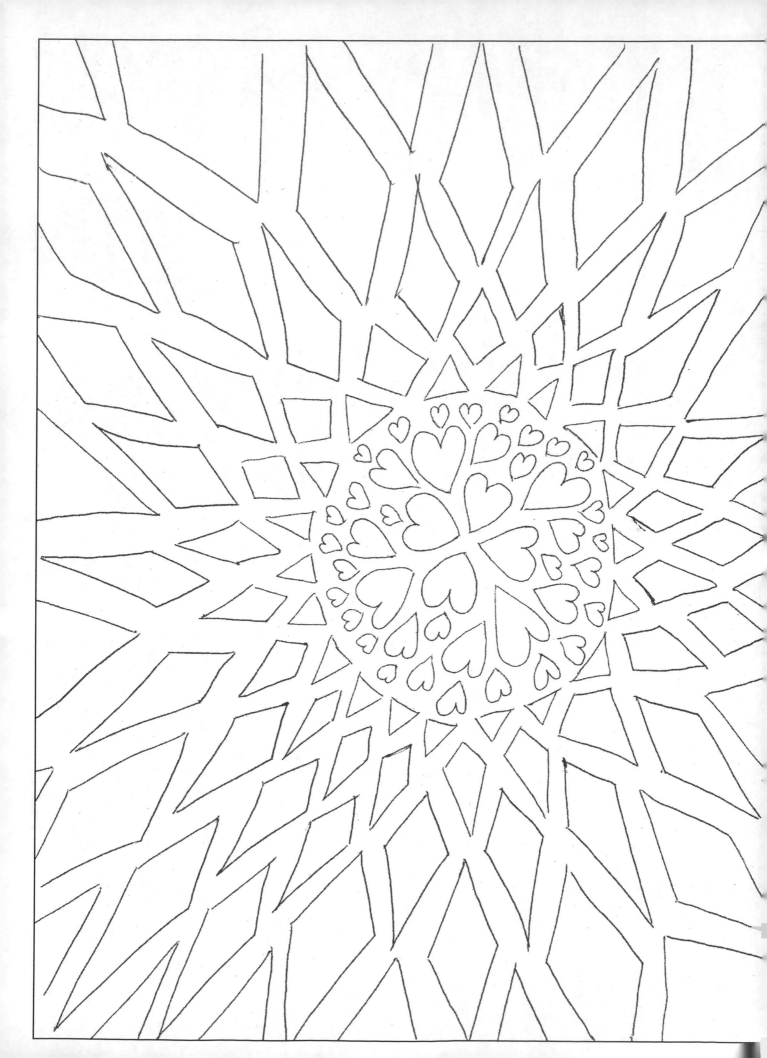

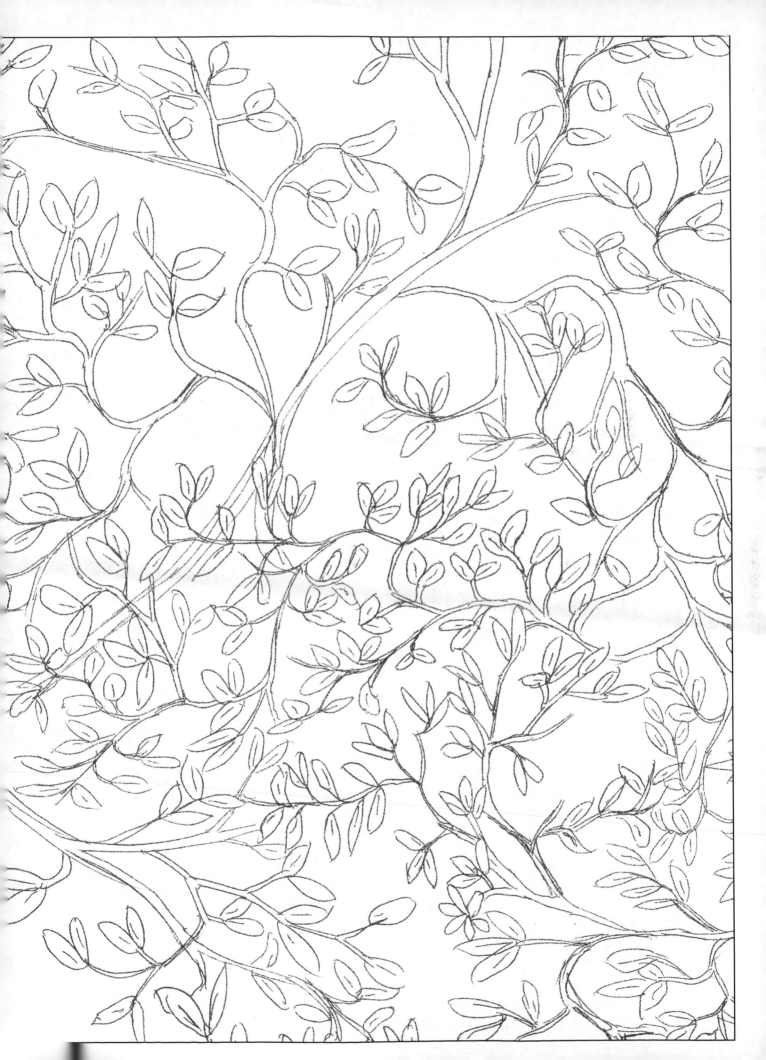

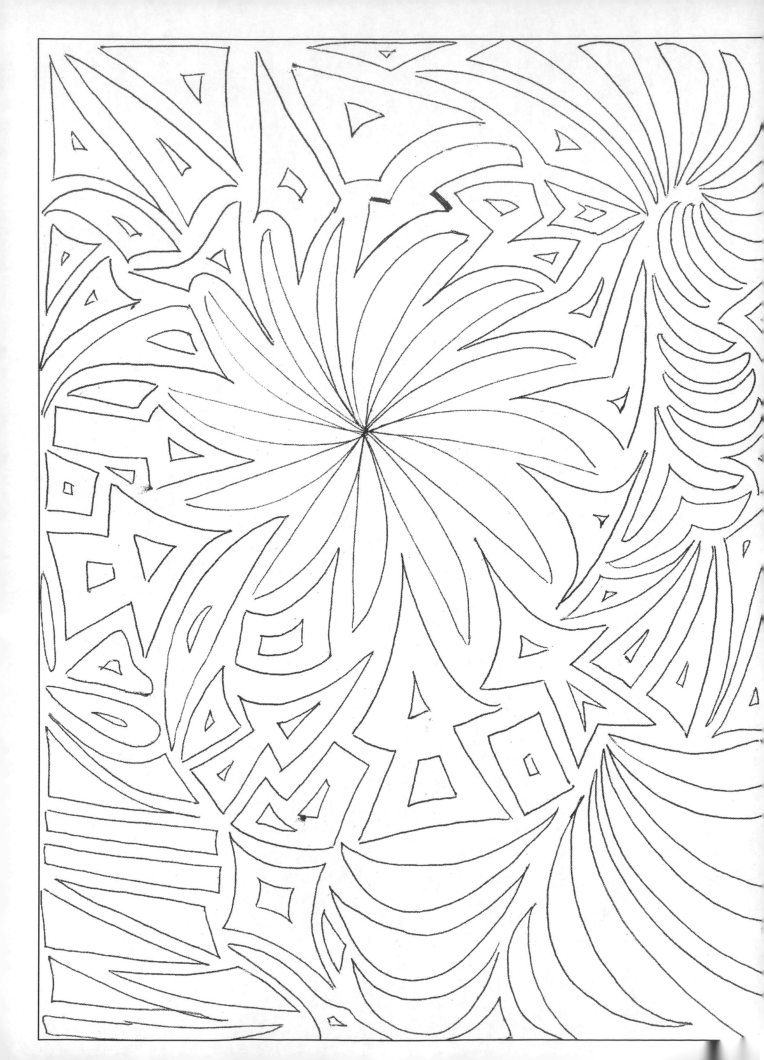

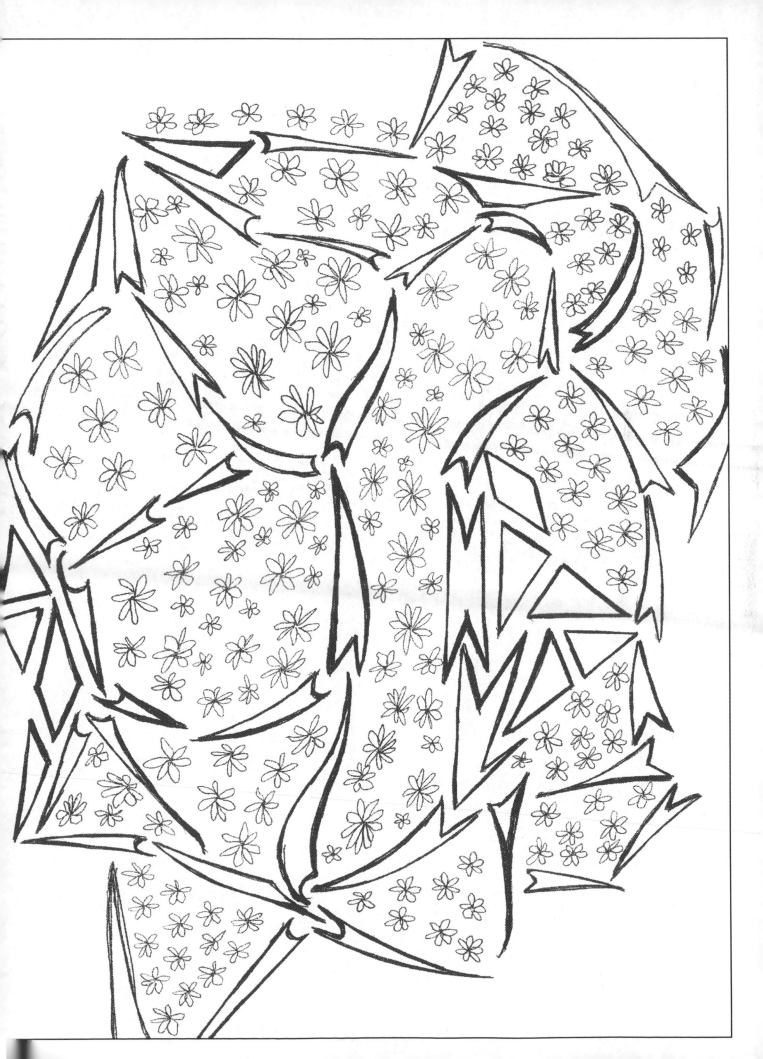

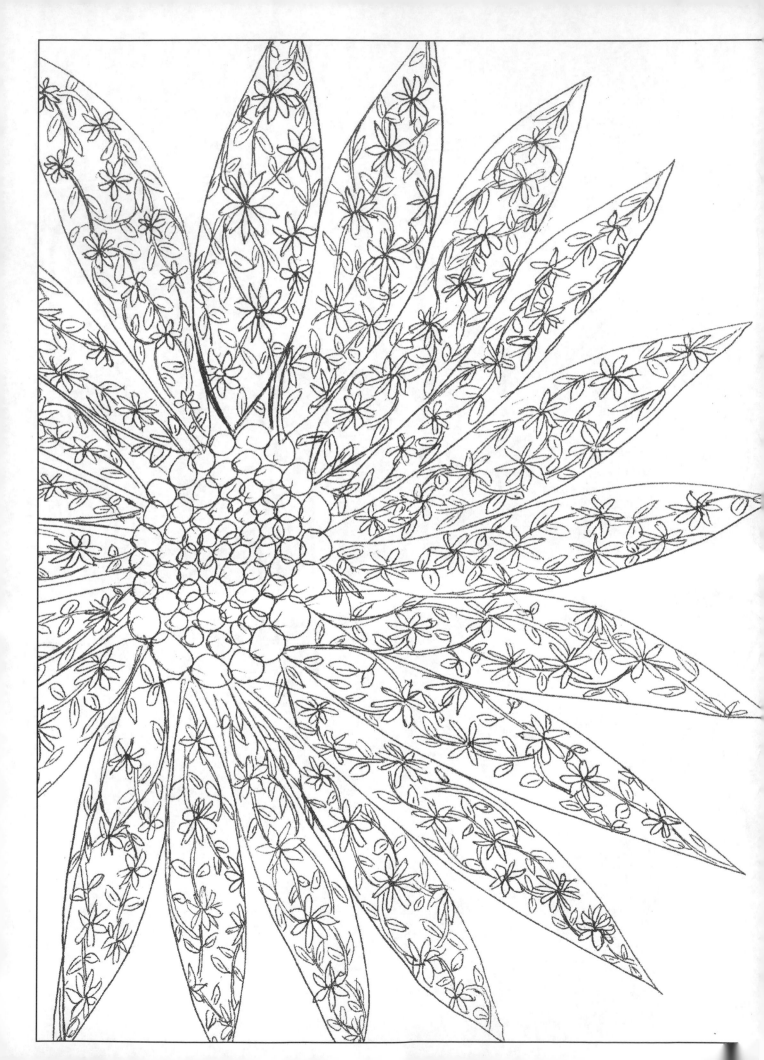

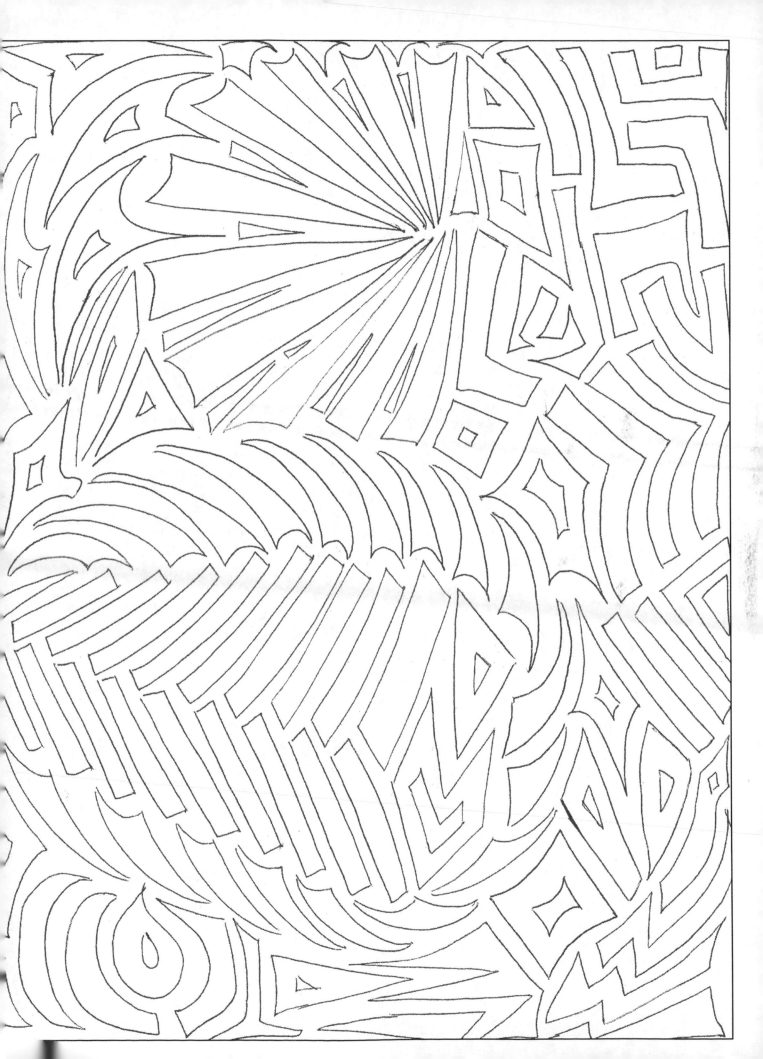

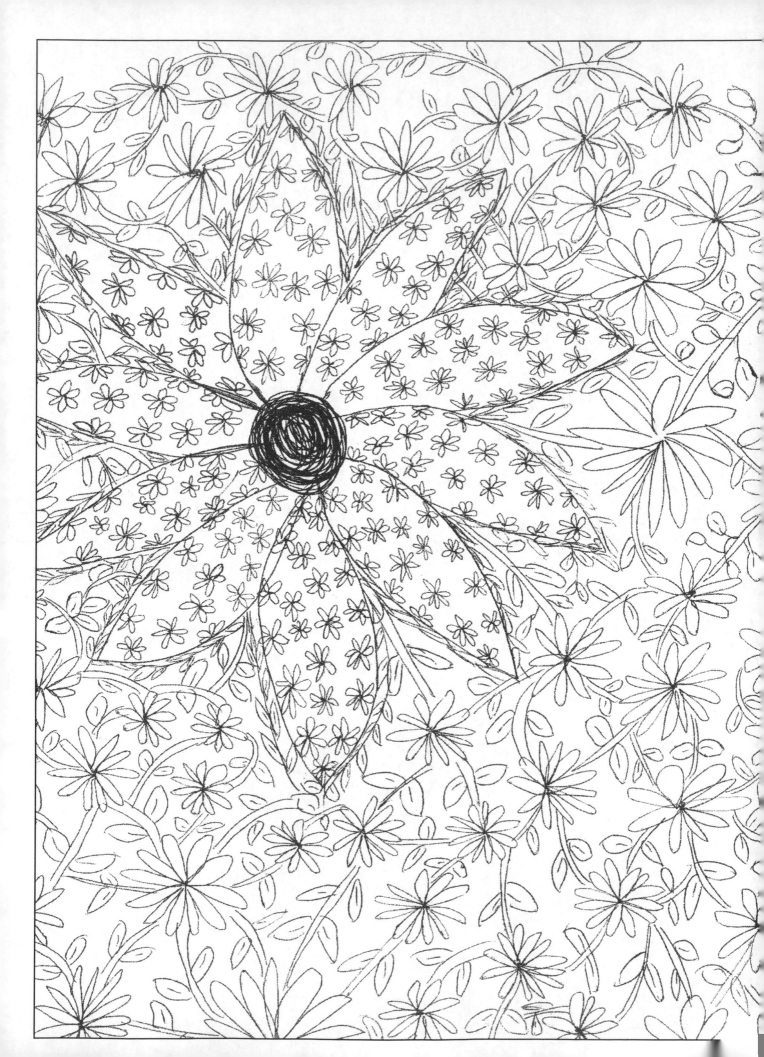

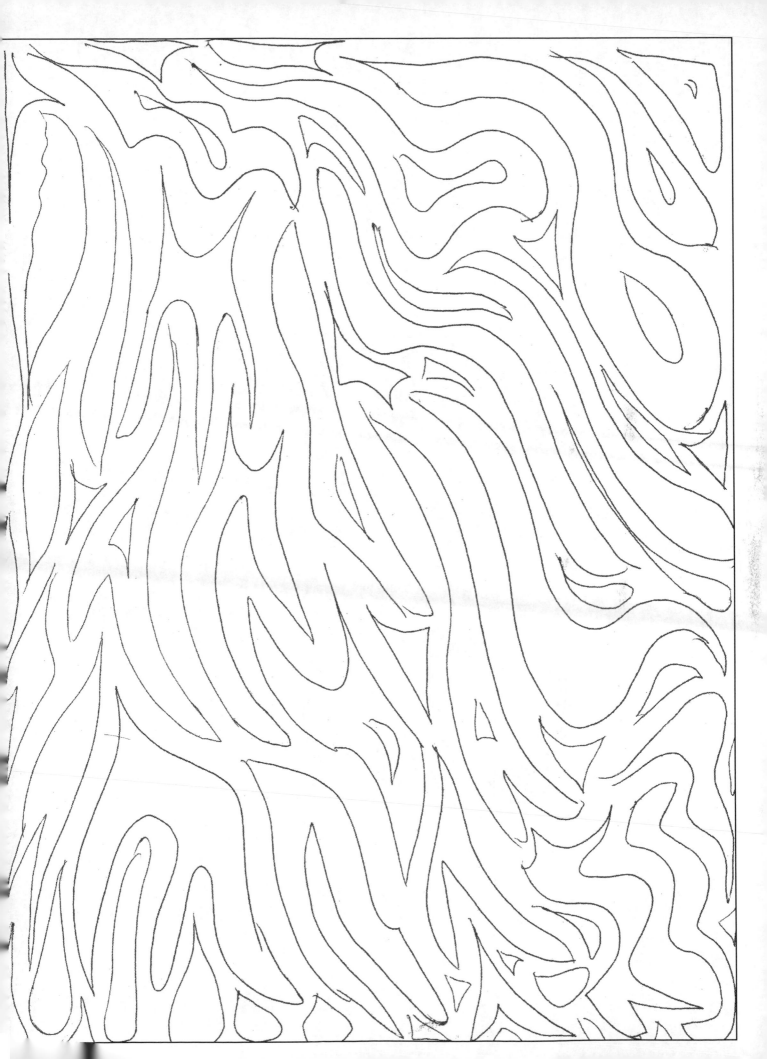

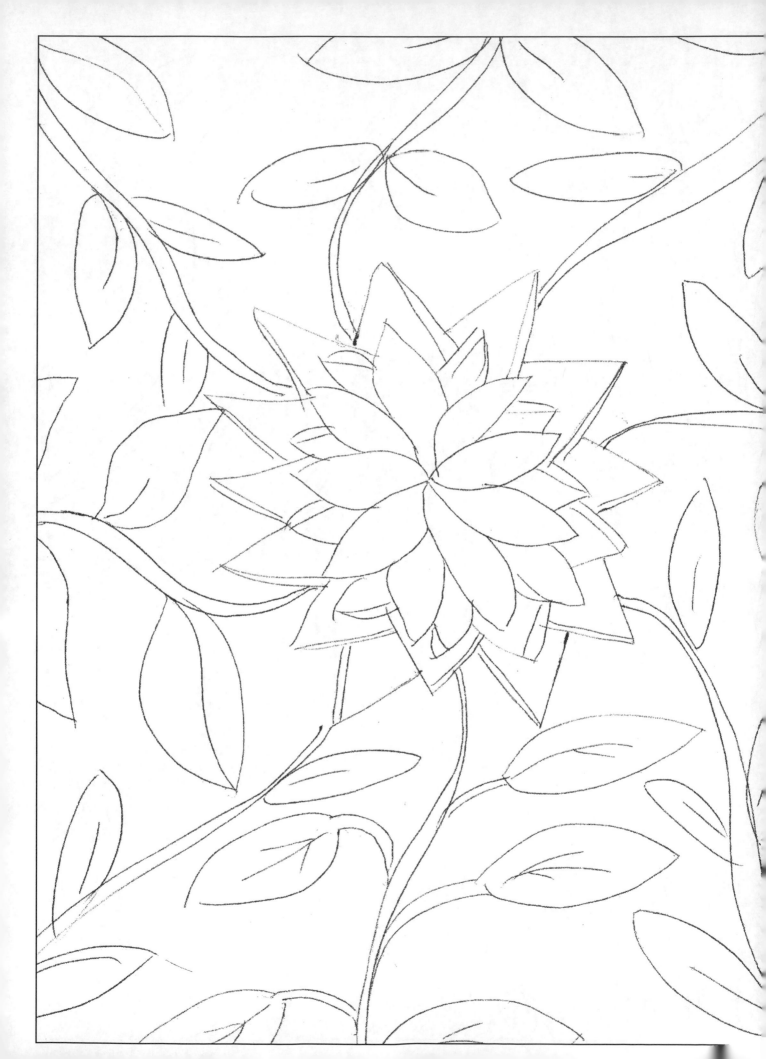

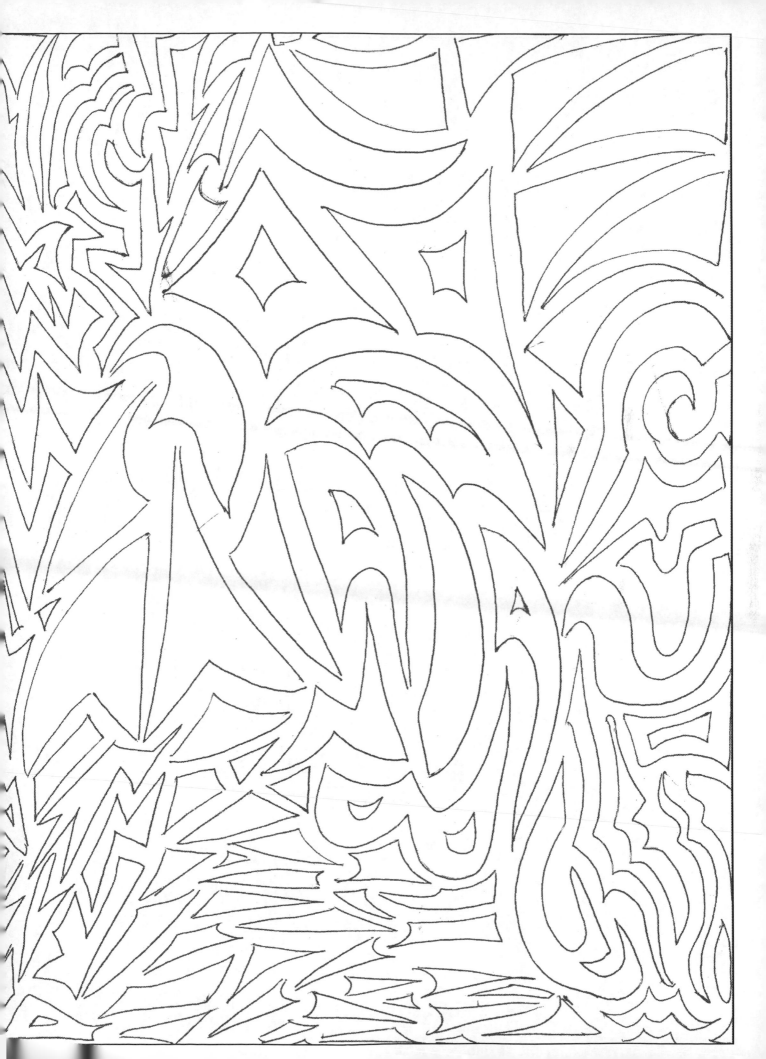

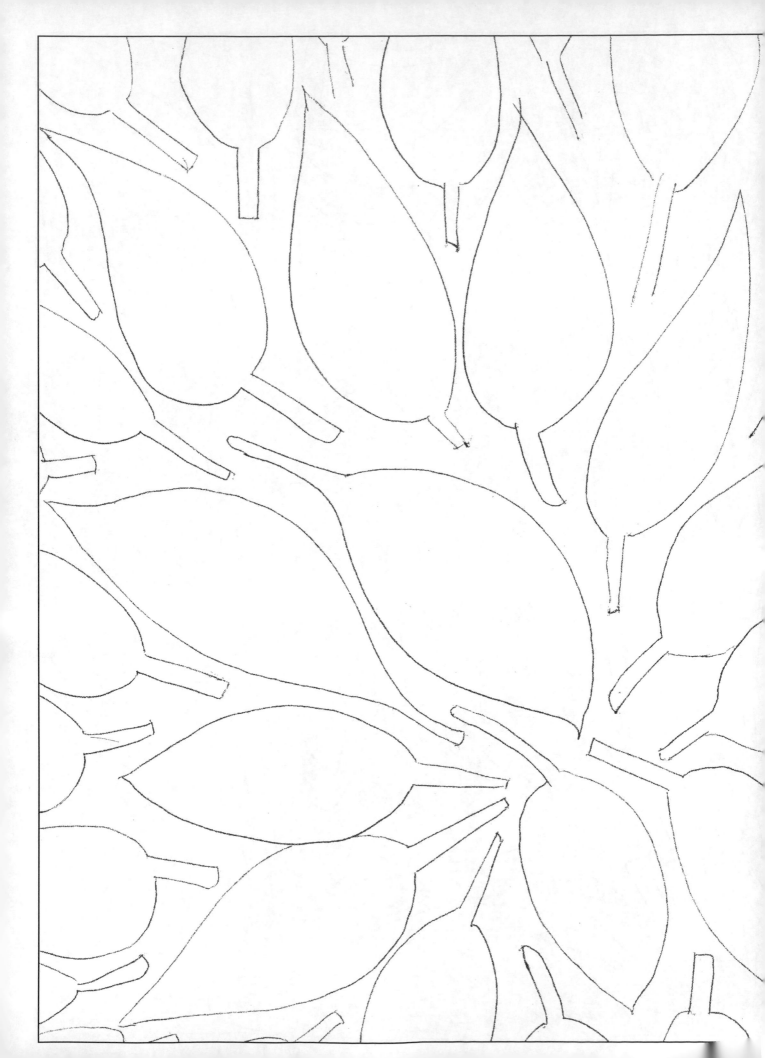

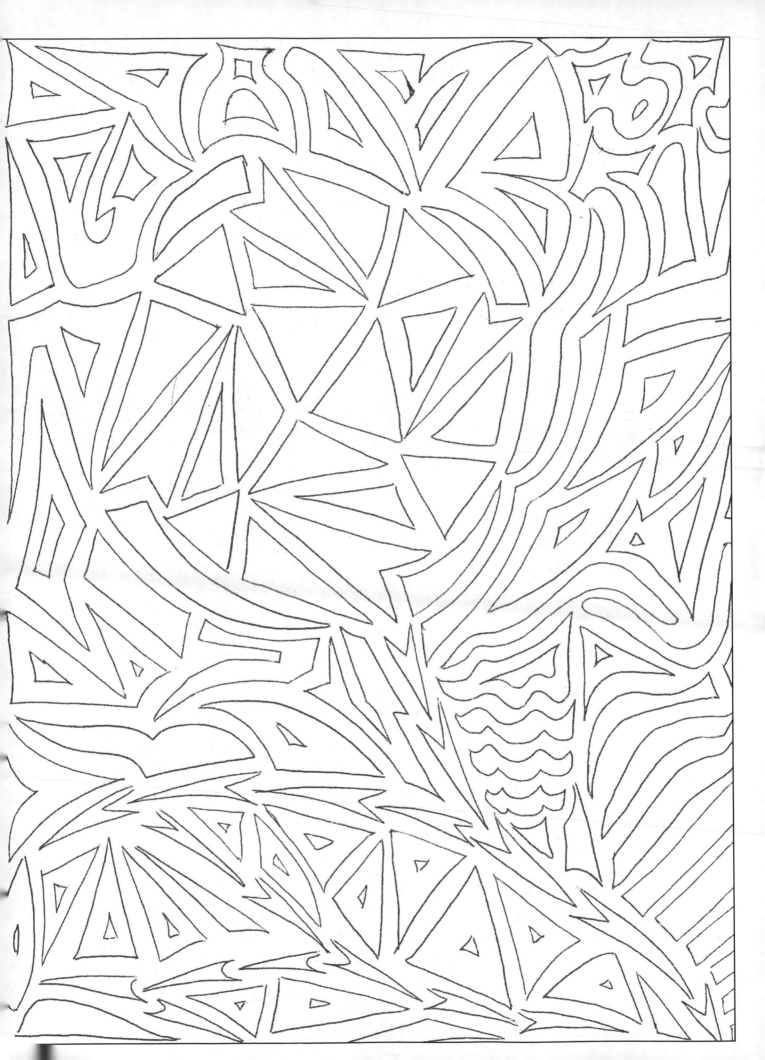

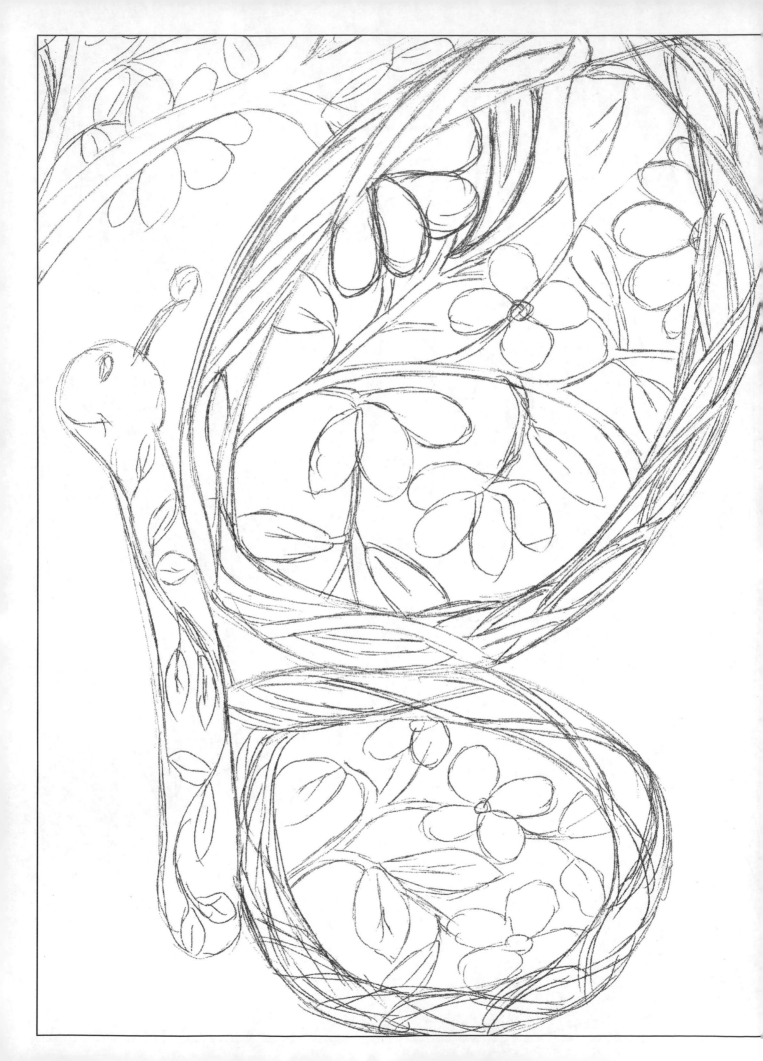

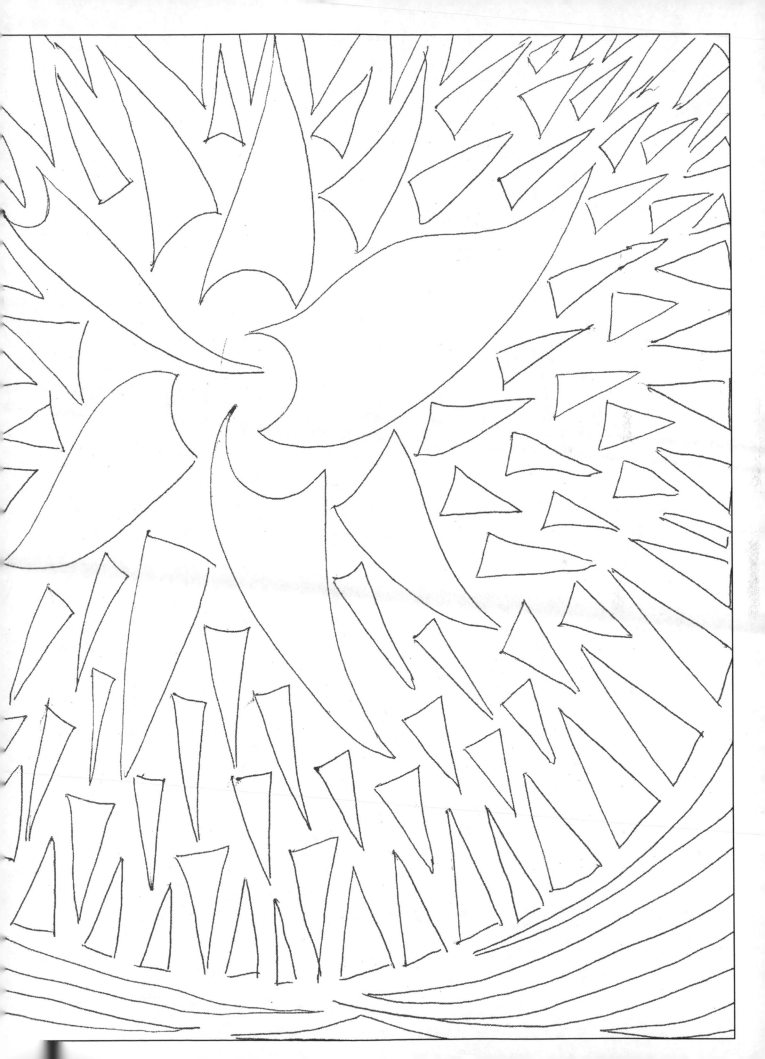

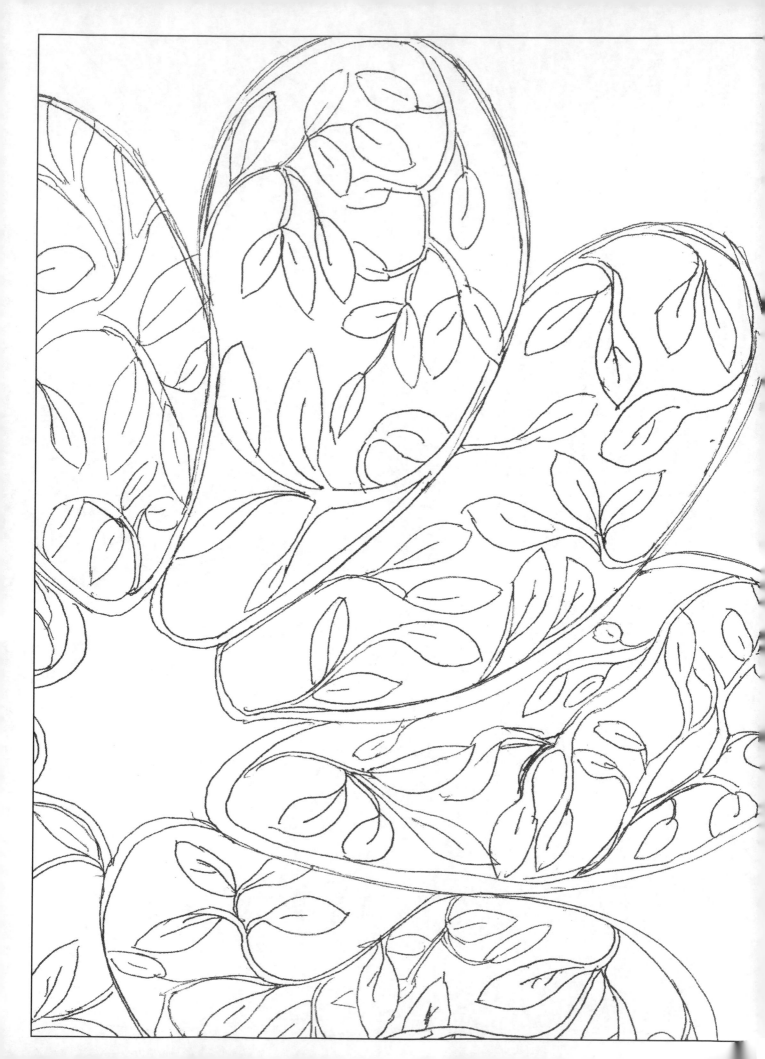

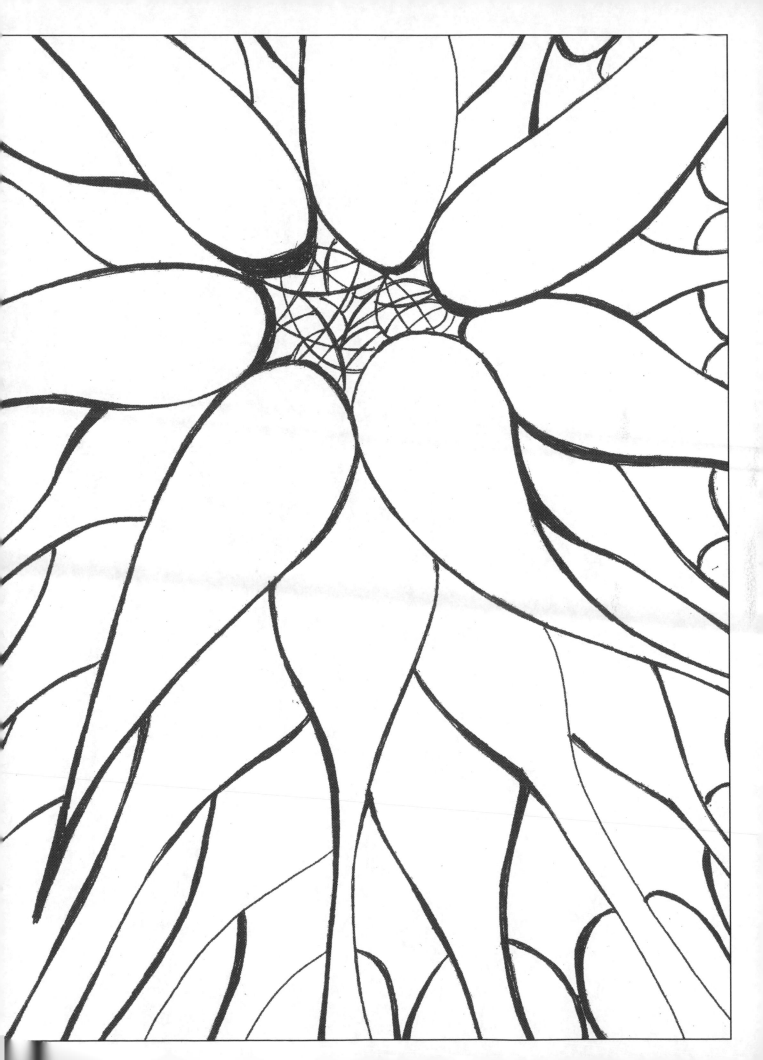

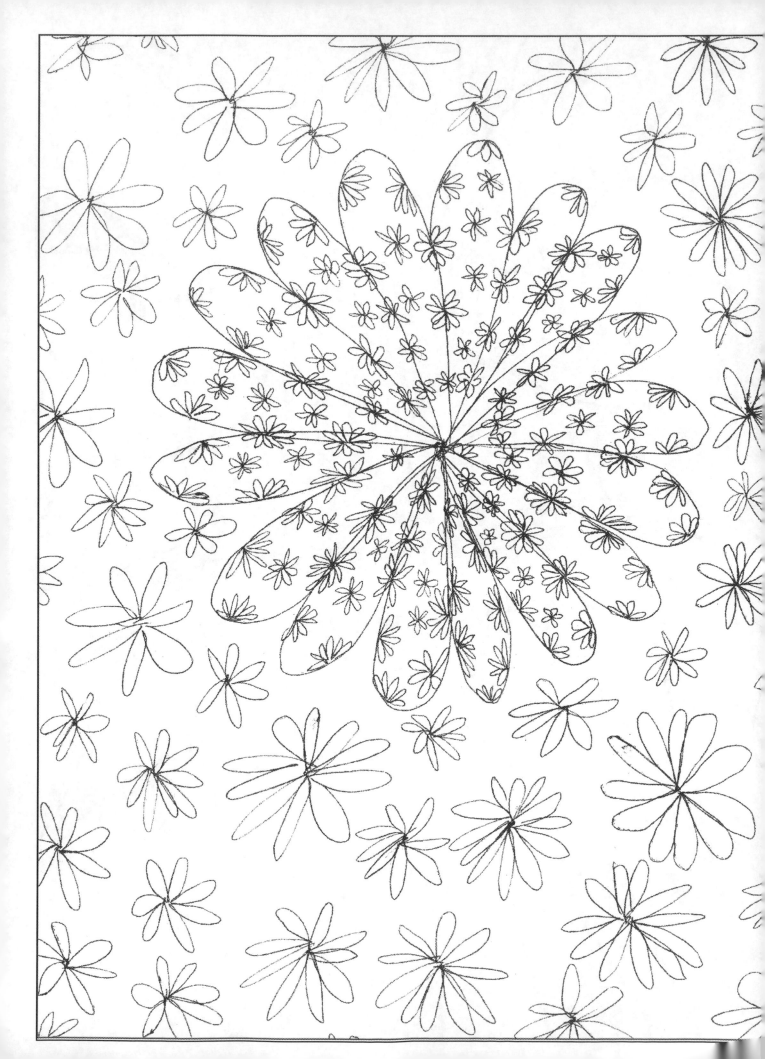

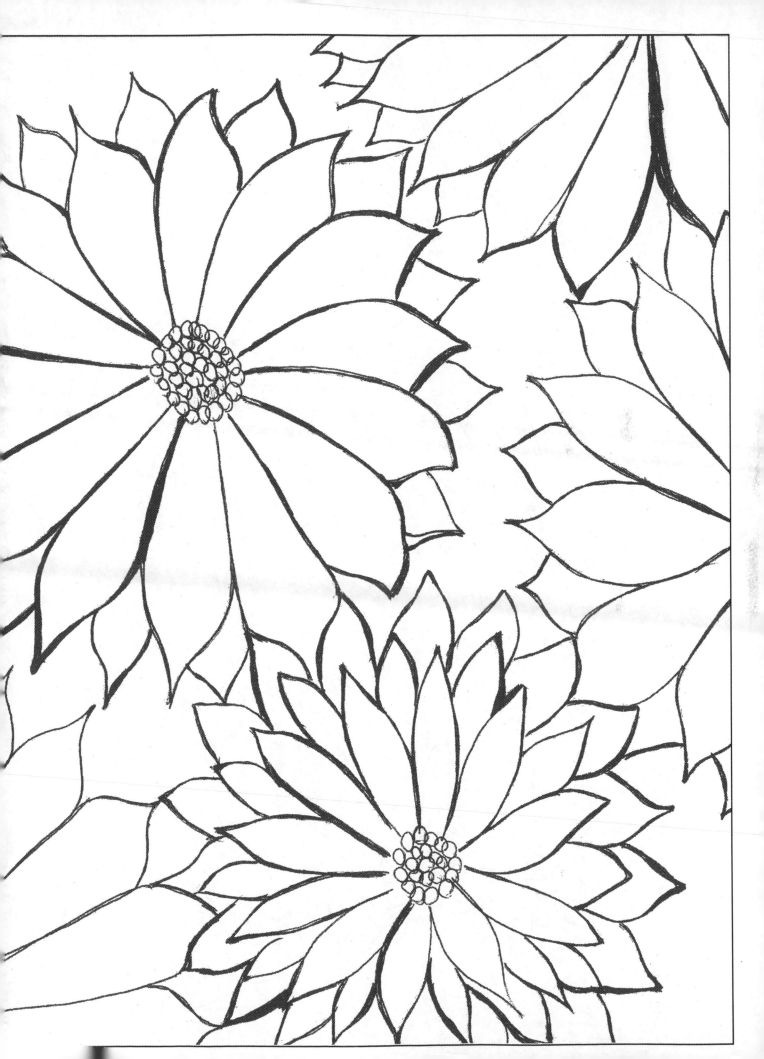

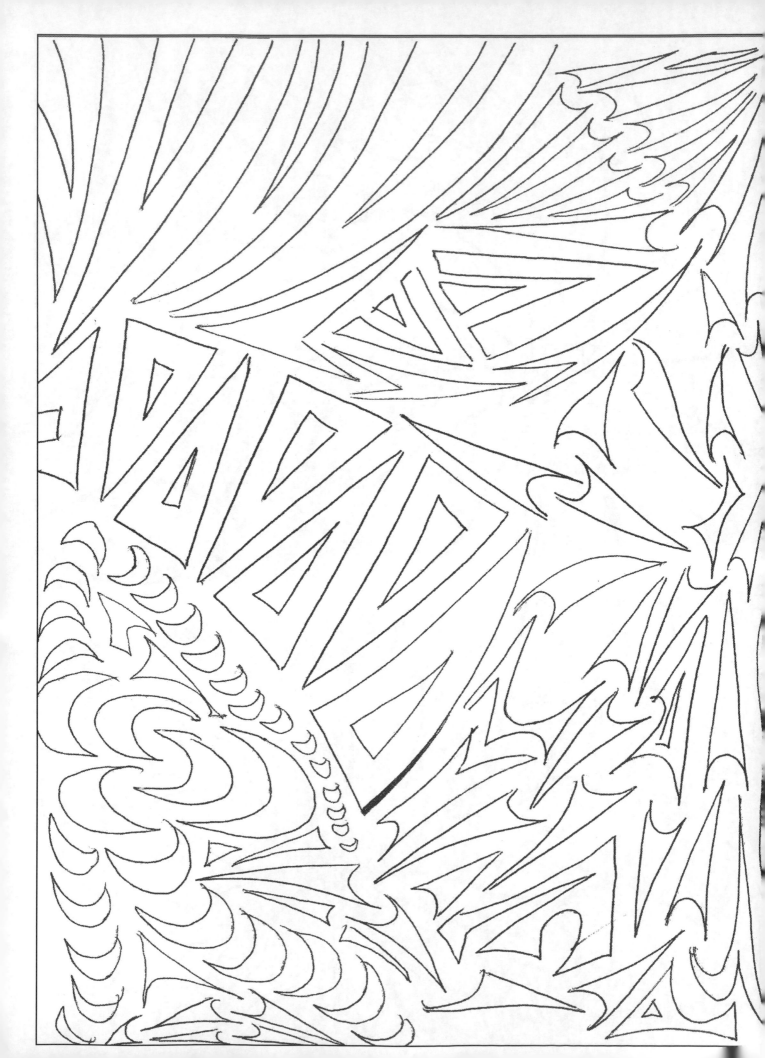

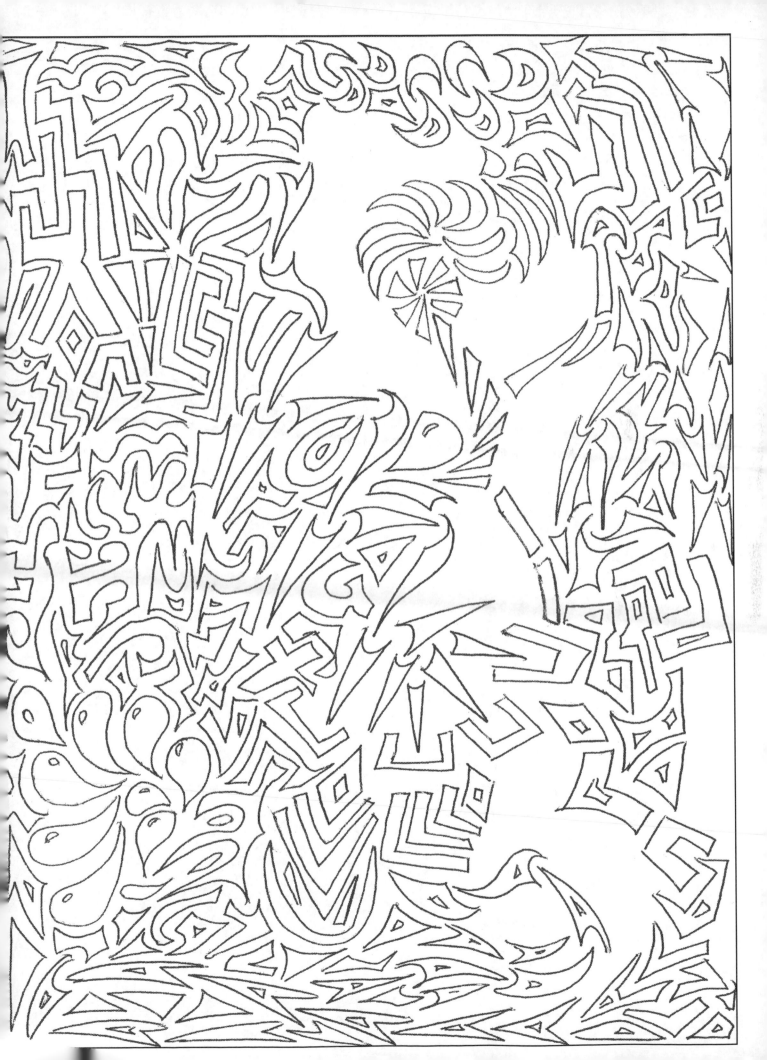

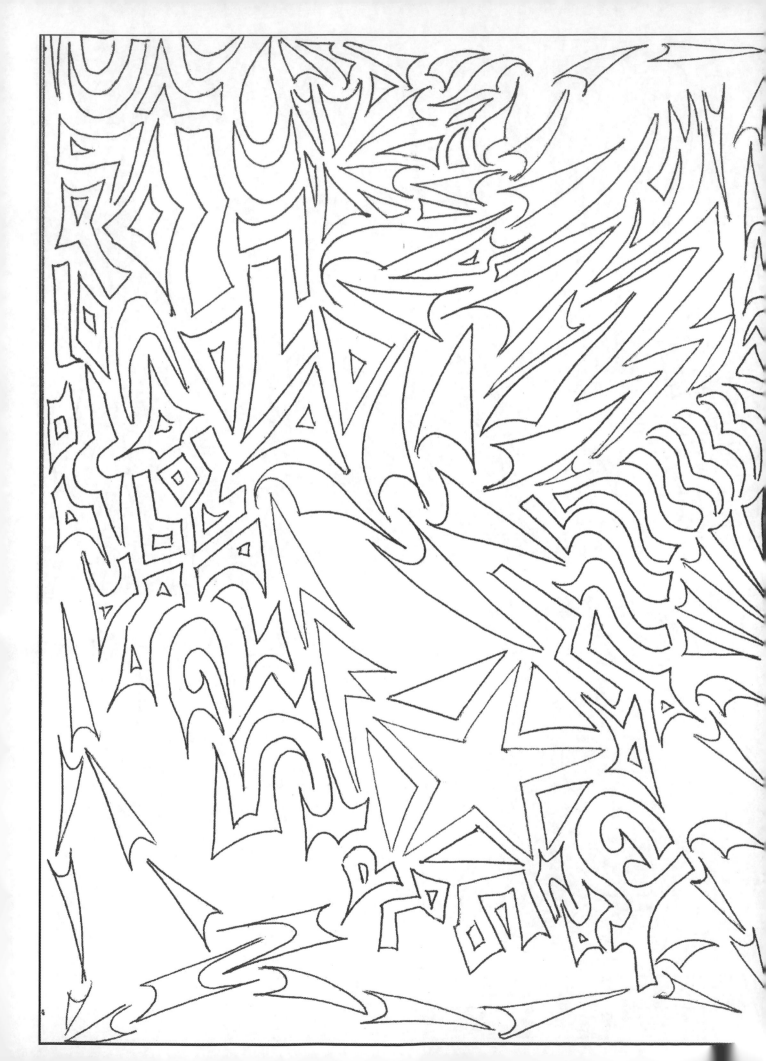

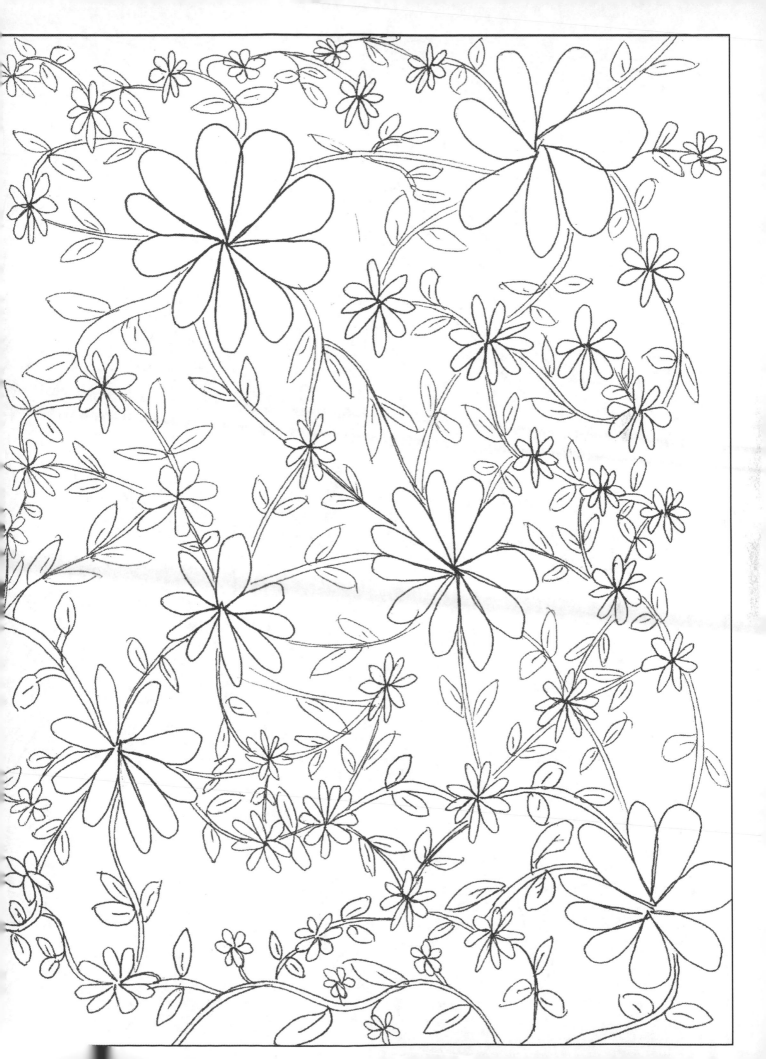

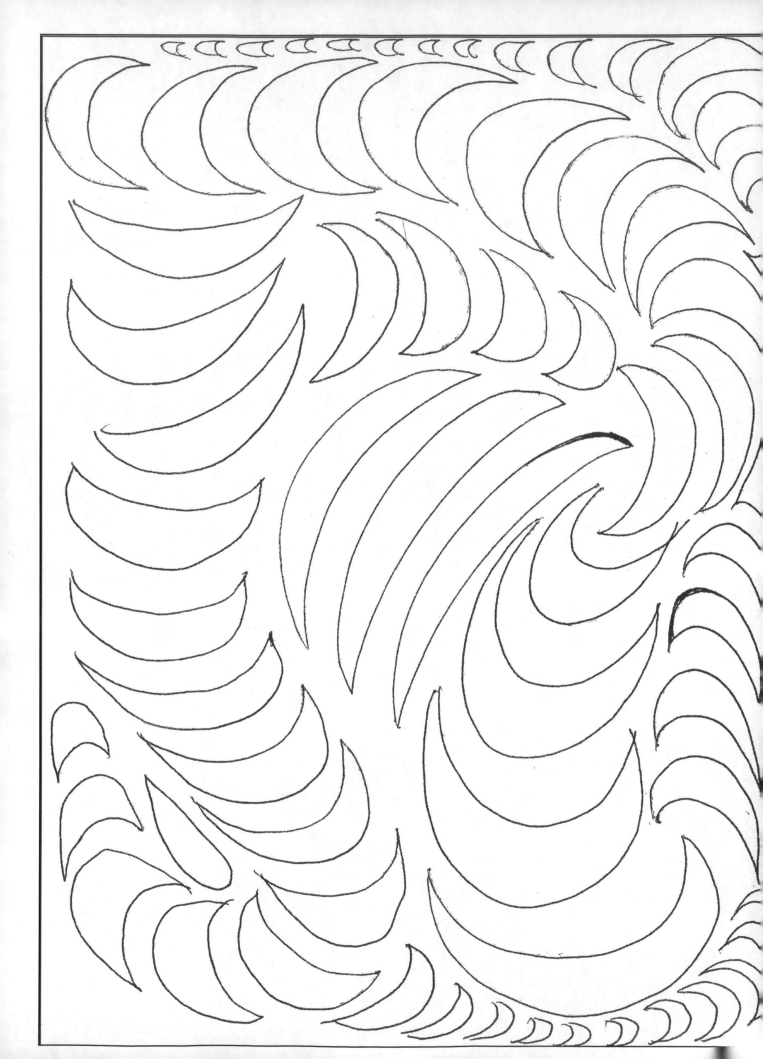

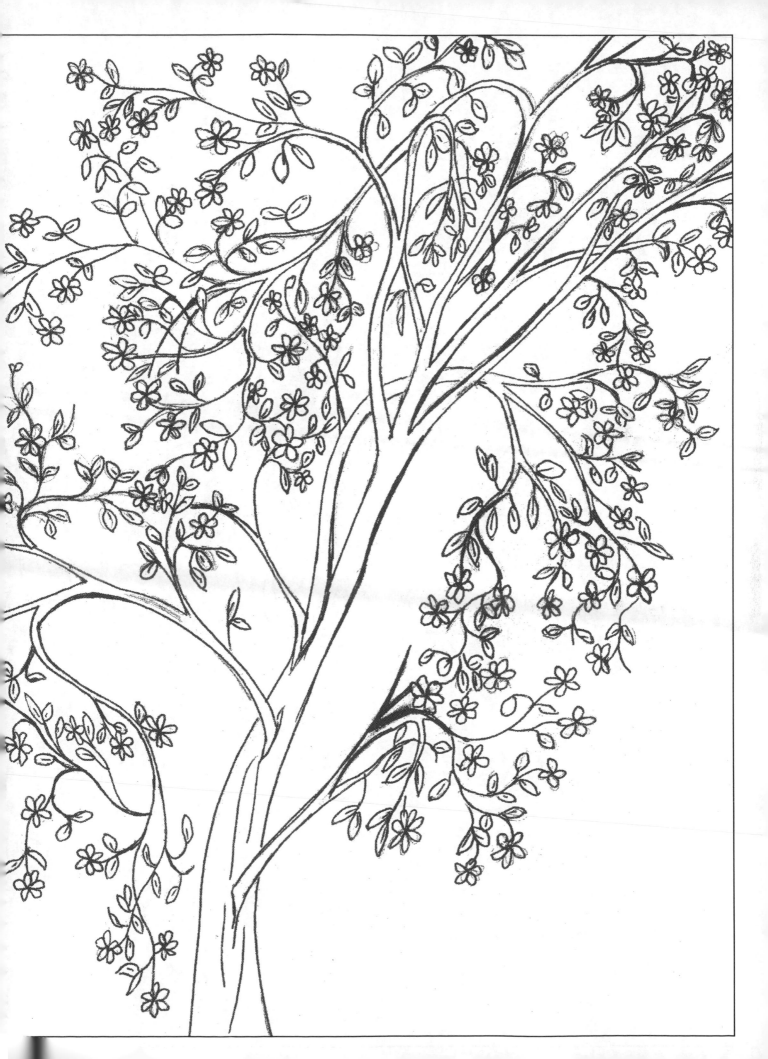

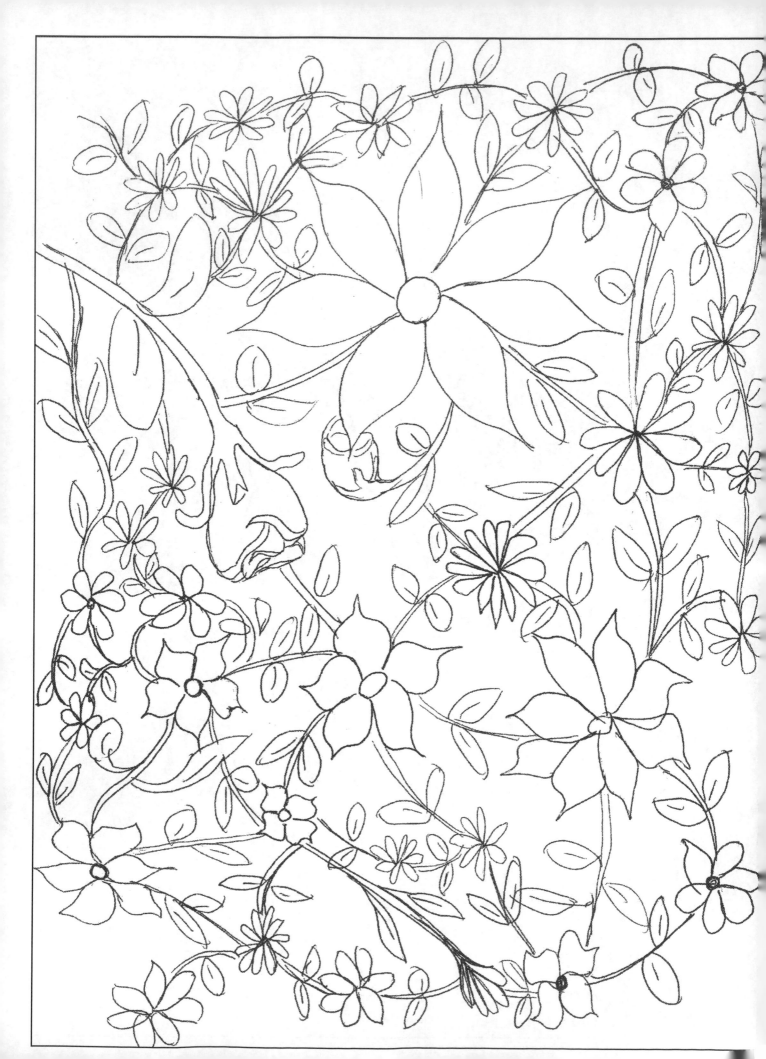

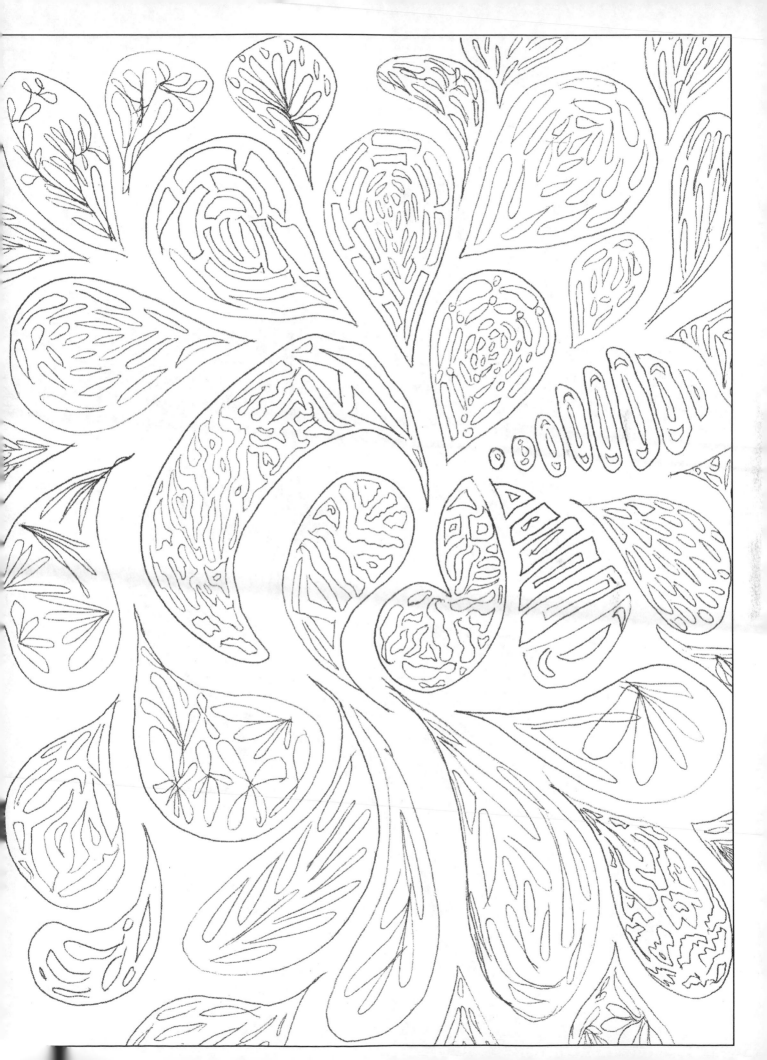

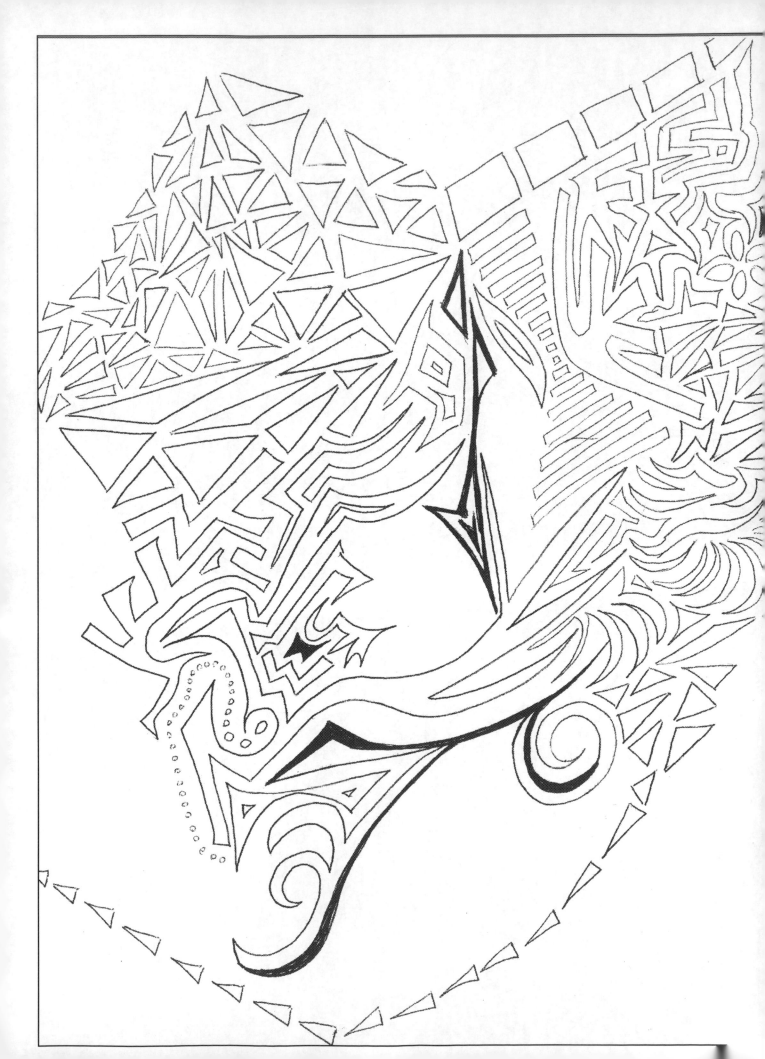

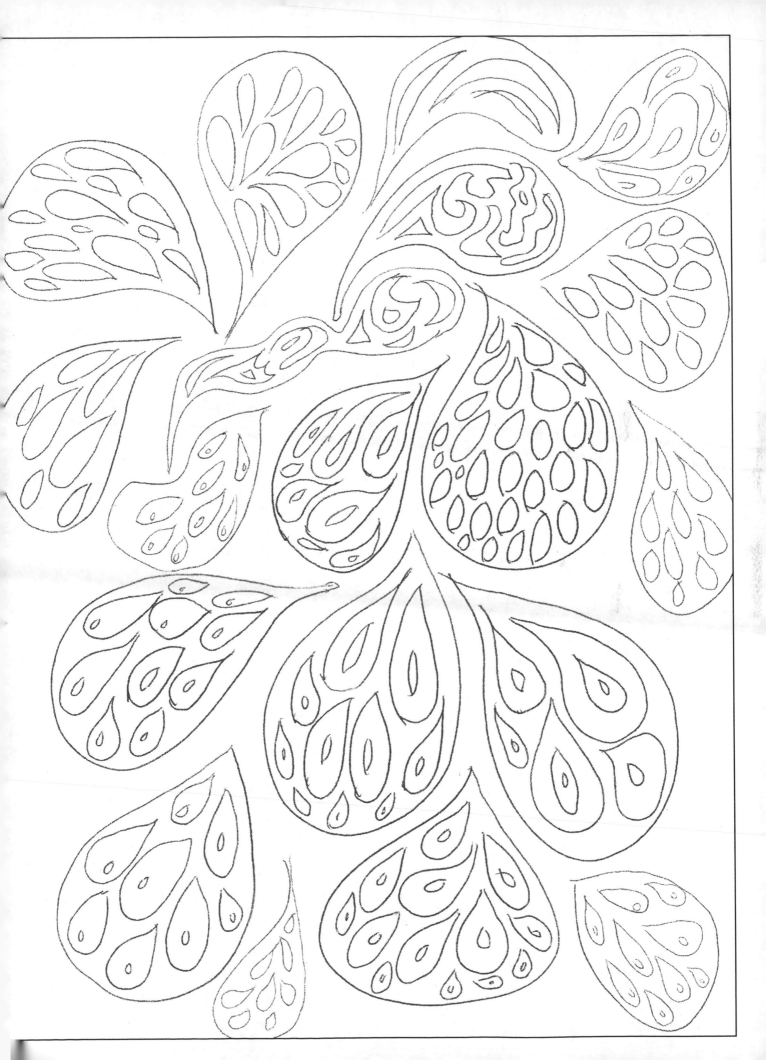

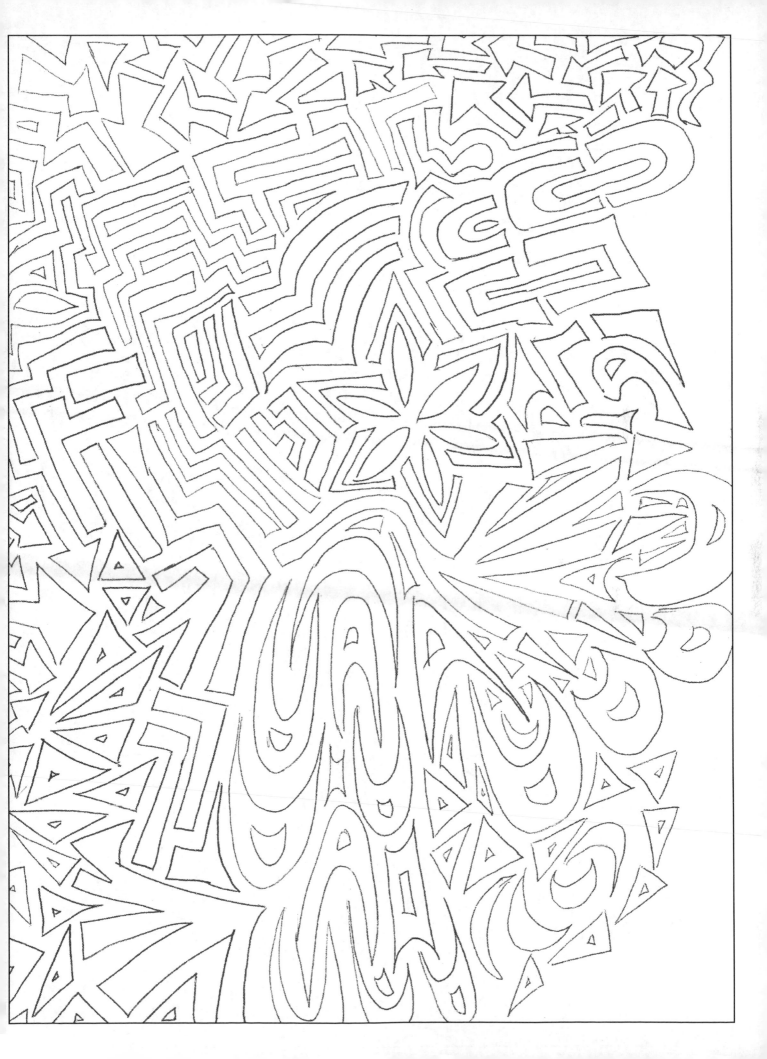

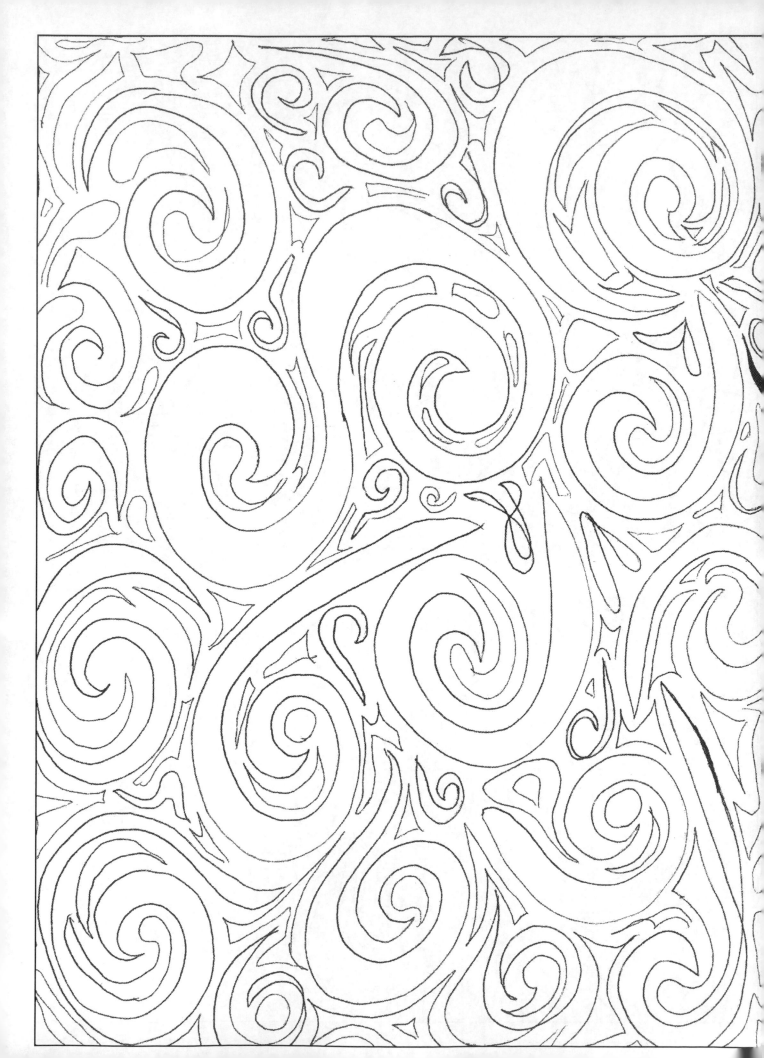

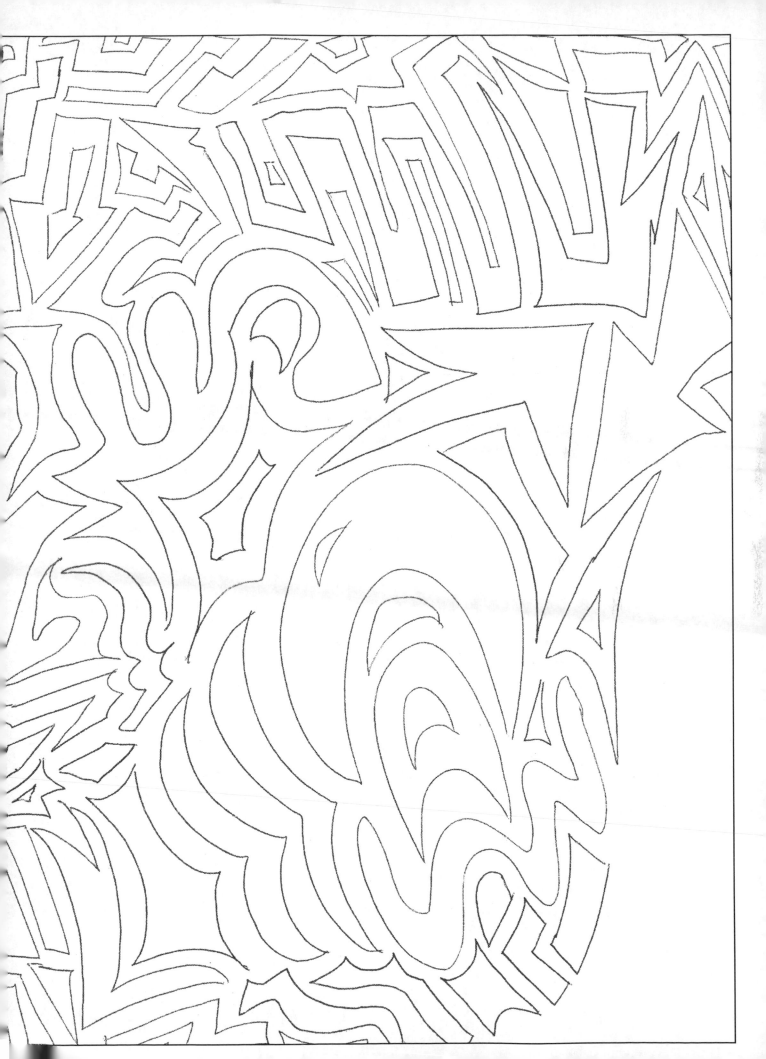

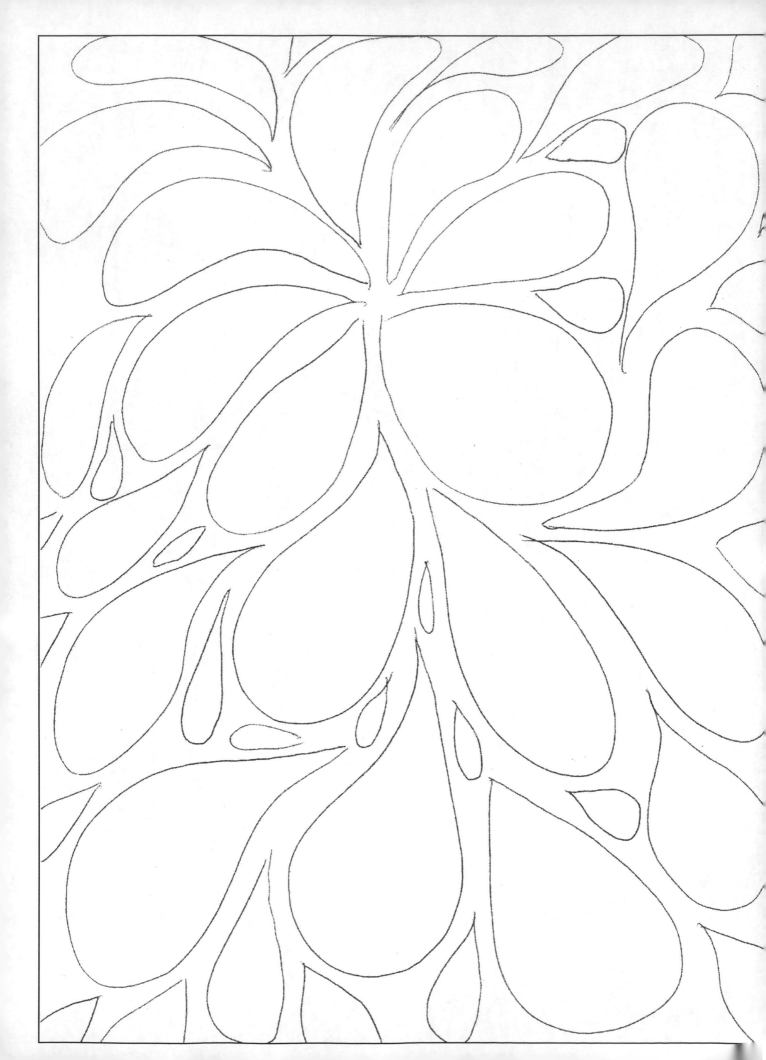

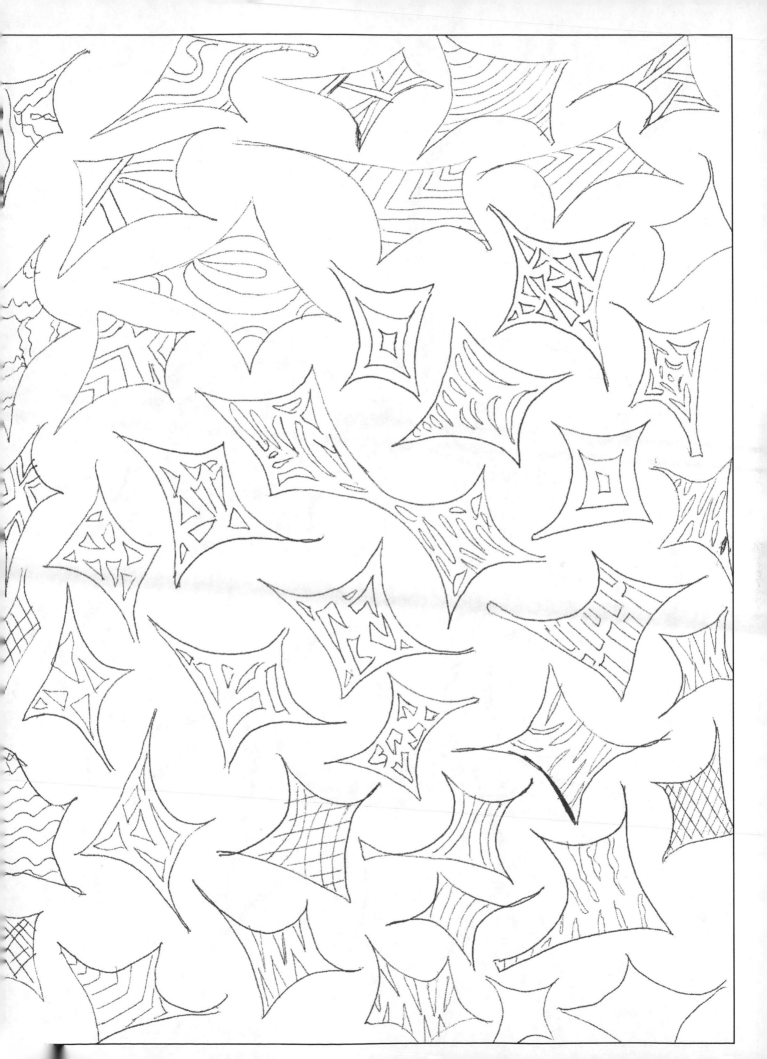

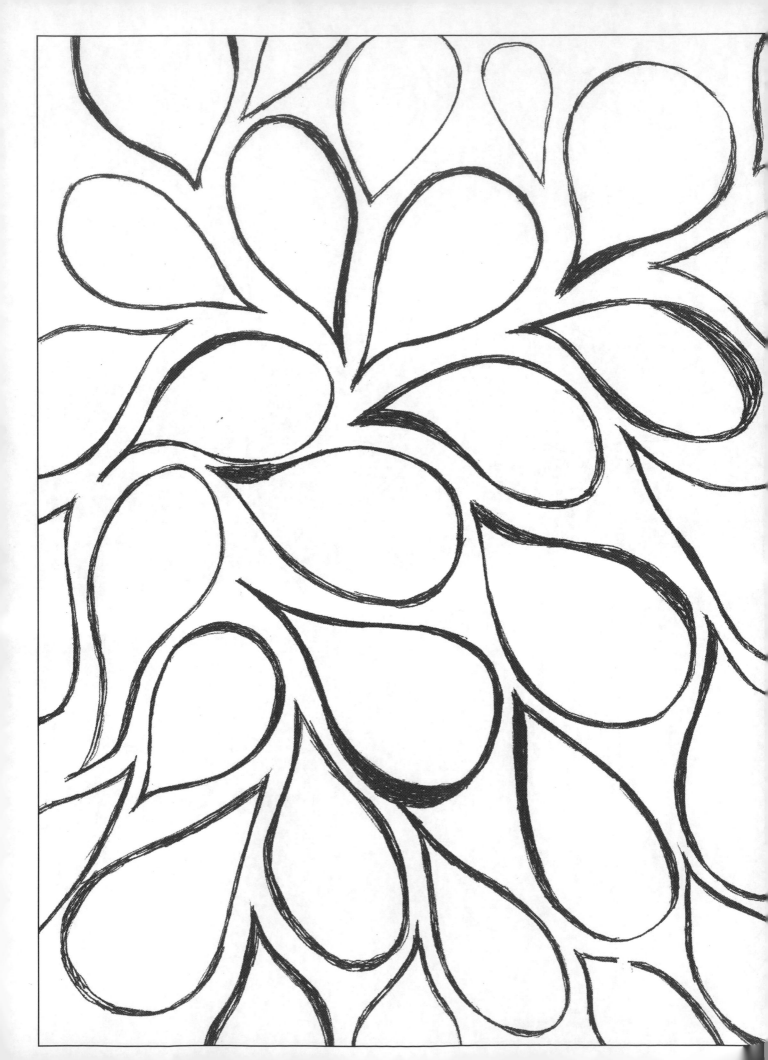

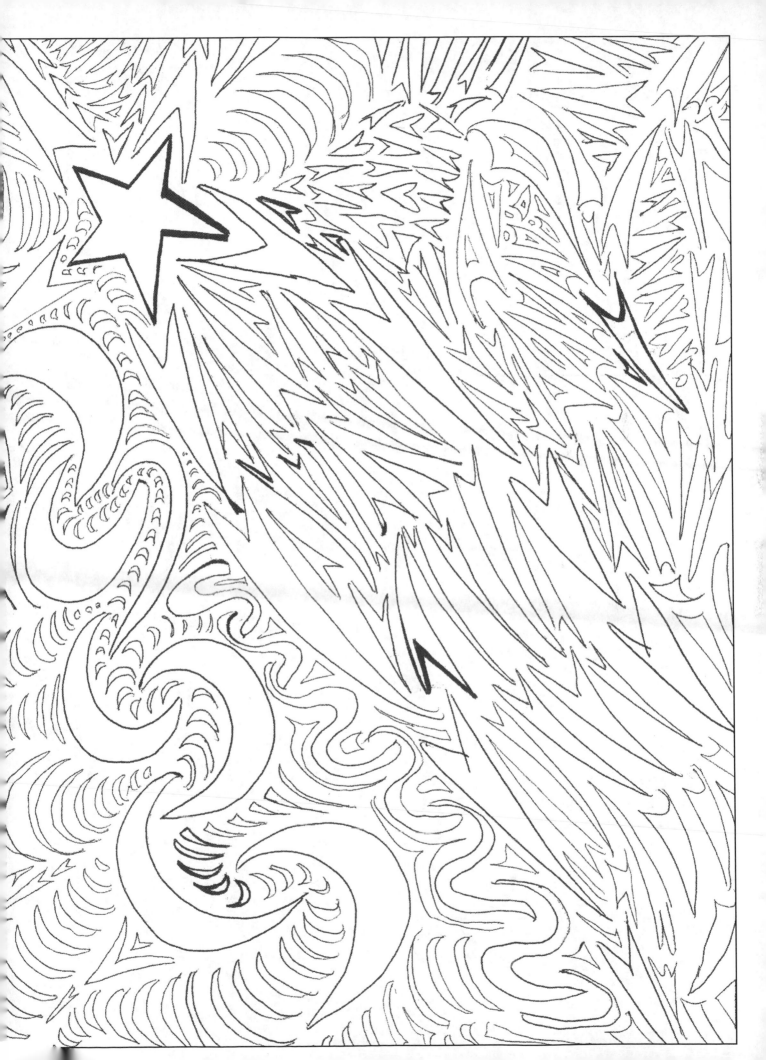

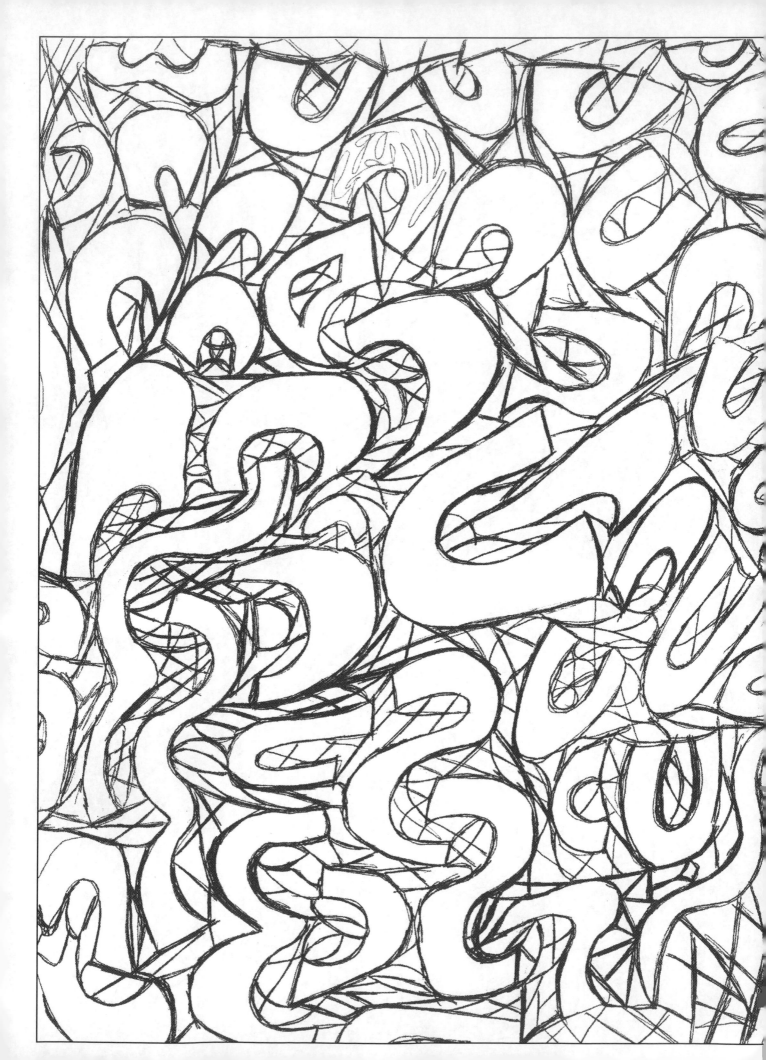